How to become a
MASONIC LODGE OFFICER

How to become a

MASONIC LODGE OFFICER

H. L. Haywood

MACOY PUBLISHING & MASONIC SUPPLY CO., INC.
Richmond, Virginia 23228

ABOUT THE AUTHOR

HARRY LEROY HAYWOOD (1886-1956) was born near Cincinnati, Ohio and was a descendant from an old English family which had helped to found the State of North Carolina. He attended two colleges, taught in a third and, during the first thirteen years of his career, was a lecturer on religion and also of anthropology.

He was Editor-in-Chief of "The Builder," the official journal of the National Masonic Research Society, for six years. The Grand Lodge of New York utilized his services for nine years, five of which he served as Editor of "The New York Masonic Outlook." He wrote exclusively for The Masonic History Company of Chicago (a firm taken over by the present publishers some years ago) during which period he produced five books and several unpublished works. In his later years he was employed by the Grand Lodge of Iowa in its famous library where he carried on research work.

Brother Haywood wrote *Symbolical Masonry*, his first Masonic book (now out of print) in 1916. Thereafter he produced many other books, one of which, *A History of Freemasonry*, in collaboration with James E. Craig, and many brochures, treatises and magazine articles. In all, he wrote more than twelve million words on the subject of Freemasonry which may exceed the output of any other writer in the history of the Fraternity.

He was an avid reader and had a prodigious memory, a scholarly background and a grasp of Masonic history, philosophy and symbolism that was phenomenal. His style is distinctive, original, unmistakable, and always readable.

Brother Haywood felt that in every Lodge there are many able, intelligent and devoted Masons, who, from modesty or lack of "know-how," have failed to qualify as officers. How well he succeds in inspiring them to do so, only the reader can determine.

FOREWORD

EVERY LODGE annually *needs* new Officers and often some of the best and ablest leadership is overlooked because of the modesty of members who are *qualified and anxious* to be of service but hesitate to offer themselves as available Officer material. This is unfair both to the members and to their Lodge.

Masonic Lodges want, need, and must have good officers.

This book shows how YOU may become an Officer of your Lodge if you can qualify. Practical suggestions of how to go about it - what the requirements are - and the proper and legitimate steps you can take to realize this laudable ambition.

The author is one of the ablest and one of the best known of Masonic writers and covers this important subject comprehensively in an entirely new and most interesting manner.

This revised edition contains a comprehensive index which we believe will be a welcome addition to a book which is as timely today as when it was first written.

The Publishers

1975

CONTENTS

CHAPTER I

PREPARATION FOR HOLDING MASONIC LODGE OFFICE

A MAN who aspires to hold office in a Masonic Lodge should not be ashamed to have others know of his ambition or hesitate to prepare himself for office holding. If you have cherished that aspiration, have you been reluctant to act upon it? If so, is it because you have been in fear of appearing too forward? There is no occasion to feel any such reluctance. Every Lodge has a continuing need for members who are interested in what the offices are, and who are well qualified, and ready and willing to undertake the work which they involve; and, instead of discouraging such brethren, Lodge officers are only too happy to welcome and encourage them.

You can, therefore, be perfectly frank and open about it, without any reservation or misgivings. You should discuss it with your Lodge friends, and with the Brethren who are now officers. If you will undertake the definite program of preparing yourself for holding Lodge office, such as is recommended and discussed in the following pages, you will be serving the best interests of your Lodge and yourself. Consider what many years of holding offices in the Lodge will mean in your own life and career: enlarged acquaintance, warm friendships, training in leadership and service! The subsequent discussion will make clear what that service will be; for a man who holds Lodge offices, one after another, must give to them much of himself, and of his time, money, and effort.

An office in a Masonic Lodge is unlike an office in any other society, organization, or fraternity; this or that about them may appear to be similar, but they are not so in reality; and they are not so for the same reason that Freemasonry itself is unlike any other society or fraternity. What a Lodge office is, belongs peculiarly to what Freemasonry itself is. No amount of service in offices in other organizations, therefore, can be taken as an adequate preparation for holding Lodge office, except merely that such training may put a man more at his ease when appearing in public, or give him a working knowledge of a few details of organizational procedure. A Masonic office is something peculiarly itself; the qualifications required by it are uniquely its own. This is because a Lodge office is not an external adjunct to the Craft, but belongs to what Freemasonry itself is. Hence if in the spirit of Masonic emulation a man has a desire for a place in the Lodge's official work, it is because he feels he would fit in just there, and in just that way. Freemasonry is much besides offices; it is teaching and learning; it is charity and relief; it is entertainment, good fellowship; it is symbols, emblems, and allegories; it is to sit on the sidelines, to discuss and decide Lodge business; but what it is in its offices, it is also in these other forms of its activities. A man cannot work in the Lodge in every one of these ways at once, but must choose for himself his place in it; and if he finds his place to be in the offices, then is he indeed fortunate.

You will have a better understanding of what a man finds in the Lodge offices if you clearly see that they are not pieces of external machinery but are themselves essential parts of what Freemasonry actually is. What would be left of the Degrees, Rites, Ceremonies if the Lodge offices were removed from them? It is not merely that there would be no means to keep them going, but rather it is that much would be lost out of what they are, in themselves; for the Master, the Wardens, and the Deacons are themselves part of the Degrees, belonging to them as do the symbols. So, also, with many other workings of the Craft, as in relief, or in entertainment, or in teaching, or training candidates, or community affairs; some office, or offices, belong of themselves to such activities. Anything that Freemasonry is anywhere, or does, has something of the Lodge offices in it. An office was made what it is because of that fact; it is furthermore because of this that no office can be altered to suit the wishes or desires of the man who is to occupy it, for to alter any one of them would be to alter Masonry, and that is impossible. A man must equip himself to fit the office as it exists, and not expect the office to be modified to fit his personality or peculiarities.

But what if it be argued that ambition to hold Lodge office is in violation of both the words and the spirit of the old adage, that "The Office should seek the man, not the man the office?" There are two answers. If the allegation is taken to imply that a Lodge office is an honor, bestowed on some popular Brother in order to give him a higher rank and title, then again it is wide of the mark. Indeed, a greater mistake could hardly be made; so far is a Lodge office from being merely an empty honor, it is something of a wholy different sort. An office is a place of service and a way of work. In no other place in Freemasonry is so much work called for, long-continued, exacting, onerous work. Browning's jibe, "Just for a ribbon to pin on his coat", does not apply to Lodge offices.

An office is not a detachable mechanism, used merely to

push from behind like an engine; neither is it automatic—and this does not abate anything just said. It consists of things to be done, to be said, to be felt, to be decided; things which only a man can do, and which no office, with the man left out, could ever do. Since this is so, then is it necessary that some man should *be* what it calls for, as well as *do* what it calls for, because the things an office requires a man to say or do demand that he have corresponding qualities of mind and heart, of character, and of personality; because without them he is unfit to say or do them. The incumbent can no more detach himself from his office than he can detach the office from the Lodge.

The Lodge offices, taken together, are so perfectly designed that it would be impossible to better them—where else in any human institution is a set of offices that have continued practically unaltered for centuries. Considered severally, in the light of their places and functions, they divide themselves roughly into three groups, though this division has no legal existence. 1. They are the Principal offices. 2. The Secretary and Treasurer. 3. The Stewards and the Tiler. Of the Principal officers of the Lodge, the Worshipful Master is chief. He is supported by a Senior Warden and a Junior Warden. They in turn are assisted by a Senior Deacon and a Junior Deacon. The Secretary and the Treasurer have certain business affairs of the Lodge to attend to. The Senior and Junior Stewards and the Tiler have a sphere which lies more outside the Lodge room proper than in it. The Principal Officers are elected by ballot once a year. The others are appointed by the Worshipful Master when he is installed. A certain number of Standing Committees are usually provided for in the by-laws, such as, Committees on Finances, on Grievances, on Charity; a certain number of special committees may be set up as need arises. The Worshipful Master usually appoints members to committees of either sort.

A Lodge itself must be a constituent member of its Grand Lodge and continue as such. Grand Lodge law requires that each Lodge must have a written Charter issued by it. The Lodge is therefore under the continuing control of its Grand Lodge; the Worshipful Master is answerable only to the Grand Lodge itself or to the Grand Master. Other than this a Lodge is sovereign in its own jurisdiction, and the Master is its head. At no time can a Lodge alter its regular offices or subtract from, or add to, their number or their duties; nor do Grand Lodge laws permit the incumbent of a Lodge office to alter it to conform to any theory of his own as to what his office should be.

Lodge offices thus have a legal status, one fixed and defined by the Grand Lodges and set forth in their laws, rules, and regulations. They have an organizational status, being the means by which Lodge members and their activities are held responsible to constituted authority. And they have a status in the administration of business affairs—for in Freemasonry, remote as it is from business or the state, dues must be levied and collected, money must be received and expended, and books and records must be kept.

But Lodge offices also have functions other than those mentioned; and though these are defined in the Ritual, the Landmarks, or in the Book of Constitutions, they are non-legal and non-administrative. When first looked at from this aspect, Lodge offices are seen to have places and functions so different from what almost everywhere are taken to belong to organization offices, that these places and functions may be described as belonging rather to some such order of things as philosophy and ethics; both of which are in all truth sufficiently remote from administration or official machinery. While, therefore, you are considering what offices are, it is necessary that you consider these other aspects also, lest you overlook matters important to your preparations.

There is in the Fraternity as a whole what some writers have called the "Religion of Masonry"; this is not the true name for it because the Craft is neither a church nor a religion, its Rites are not sacraments, its teachings are not a theology, and each member is urged to adhere to whatever religious faith he has chosen for himself. Many Masons prefer to describe it as the "Symbolism of the Craft" because that which the phrase "religion of Freemasonry" was intended to denote, is in fact better denoted by the word Symbolism. A Symbol is an object, device, design, or some word or action which represents something other than itself; and it is thus chosen because it has something in itself which unmistakably denotes, or points to, that other thing which it represents. What of the offices? Are they in the Craft's symbolism? Yes, and they are so not in spite of what they are, but because of what they are. Consequently a man who hopes to hold an office must prepare himself to have a part in a symbolic ceremony, and to be himself employed as a symbol.

The Operative Masons employed in the erection of a church or a cathedral had a room of their own, which was both a Lodge room and a work room. During the hours of labor, fifty or a hundred men might be busy in it; therefore it was necessary to have a large room, sometimes a separate building. When, at the beginning of the day, the men had to meet together to discuss as a body some new task to be undertaken, or when they met together at night to consider their own concerns, they met in the same room. The same officers presided over them when at labor and when assembled together as a Lodge. The Lodge room was headquarters; the Masons reported to it when coming to work and when leaving work, received their instructions there; made their reports in it; it was the center from which all activities radiated; the officers had responsibility for whatever was done anywhere in connection with the building.

The Craft's first rule was that the workroom must be in order. No aimless running about was tolerated; no chatter or confusion; the men remained in peace and harmony among themselves; and this held for the men who worked in the quarries or elsewhere outside the building under construction as much as for men inside. Each officer had a fixed place or station of his own; the Worshipful Master in the East end of it, the Senior Warden on the West side, the Junior Warden on the South, the Secretary and Treasurer each in his own corner, the Tiler without the entrance. In consequence each station became of itself a headquarters for the duties and activities over which the officer presided. Whatever had to do with the direction of the body of Masons as a whole, with the superintendence of the building, or with rules, regulations, and laws, centered in the East. All matters having to do with where a man worked, at what sort of task, and with what tools, centered in the West. All matters having to do with the men when not at work or not in the Lodge's assemblies, at the noon-hour, or at the end of the day, centered in the South. And so each sort and kind of activity centered in a place of its own, which was the station of the officer in charge of it, and that station had a place of its own in the room.

If, therefore, an Operative Mason paused to think about an office, what it was in itself, what it represented or embodied in Freemasonry, the idea of it was there before him, clear and plain. In the office of Worshipful Master

was the idea of headship, of the executive, of final jurisdiction and authority; it was a means by which the whole
number of workmen could be held together and directed
as a single body. In the office of Senior Warden was the idea
of the orderliness of work; in work, as a whole, are many
particular kinds of work; and each man must be employed
where he is assigned, and at the kind of work for which he
is qualified. In the office of Junior Warden was the idea
that Masons when not at work, between tasks, or at the end
of the day, continued to be Masons, and continued to be
under the rule of peace and harmony. In the office of
Deacon was the idea that each center or place of work was
in continuous relationship with every other center; one
office had to send reports, information, or instructions to
another, to the end that all of them, working in general,
would keep the work going forward as if a single man were
doing it. The Operative Mason could in this manner think
about each and every one of the offices, one after another.

The Lodges of that period ceased after a time to be
Operative and became Speculative. The nature of the
Lodge, however, remained unchanged. The Operative
Masons had a few offices which we do not have. We have
one or two which they did not have, but the nature of the
offices remains the same. While a Worshipful Master is
no longer the executive head of a body of Freemasons daily
employed at work on a building, he is still the executive
head of a body of Freemasons. This is true of each of the
other offices in the Lodge; and if you think out what any
office is now, you will find, as did the Operative Freemason,
that each one is the center of a certain kind of work, of
activities, and of duties.

When, therefore, you are preparing to hold a Lodge office, you need to understand the kind of activities of which
you would be the center. To understand that kind is to

be in readiness for anything that may arise. There are not in an office a fixed number of routine duties which could be learned by rote, for a Lodge itself is a living and active body of men; new things are therefore always arising, and one of these new things might come to your attention in that office to be dealt with or to be decided about.

If each office in the Operative Lodge room was the center of activities belonging to one kind of work, it was necessarily also a Station; that is, it had a permanent place, or site, in the room, and that site was never moved. The Master was always stationed in the East, the Senior Warden in the West, and Junior Warden in the South, and if they had not been, then the various forms of work would have clashed and conflicted, and the workmen would have been in confusion. What was true then also is true now. Freemasonry would become changed in what it itself is if the offices ceased to have each one a fixed place of its own; for, if all sorts of activities were carried on here, there, or everywhere, and at the same time, it would become impossible to carry on the work of the Lodge. Therefore, when considering what it would mean to you to hold an office, it is necessary for you to consider what it would mean to occupy a station, a fixed place. In doing so, there are two points of importance to keep in mind. First, it belongs to a Station that it will always be there, and that regardless of whether it is busy or not, the incumbent must remain there in it, and not go moving about, or let his attention wander here or there, even though he may have nothing to do for a time; and that demands patience, and also a sense of dignity which does not degenerate into fidgeting, and conversations in whispered asides. Second, to occupy a Station requires also that a man shall have, in his own understanding, the whole of its activities. He must do so because, in so many instances, he himself must decide matters that arise at or in connection with his Station or place.

If each office is a Station, then certainly the offices taken together are not a "line." Would that this absurd term had never come into our ways of speech! For to be "in the line," if it meant anything, would mean that the offices in themselves do not count, that only the officer counts, and that if he has a path to his own goal he is satisfied. There should be no such officers in any Lodge; it is not assumed that a man can be such a hypocrite for five or six or seven years. A man does not become a Senior Deacon merely *in order* to become later a Junior Warden; he becomes one solely in order to be a Senior Deacon. As far as an incumbent is concerned, while occupying a given Station there might as well be no other; he is not to sit there in expectancy of going on to another place, because it is not for him to decide whether he is to go to another place. That is for the Lodge to decide; moreover his office is not a moving escalator but a Station, and he is stationed with it.

Therefore, if you are preparing yourself in hopes of holding a given post in the Lodge (and it is to be hoped that you are), it is the part of wisdom to keep your eyes fixed only on that office and not to have your thoughts wander beyond it. For if, in example, you are not to be a Junior Warden in full reality, what are you to be? Would you be a Senior Warden later on in any truer sense? If it were to be argued that, as a matter of fact, the Craft has the custom of "advancing" a man from an office to the one next above it, and has had it from time immemorial, the answer is that this is not promotion or given as a reward, but belongs to another order of things in Freemasonry. For it is one of the ideas in it to have a man prepare himself at one post to do the more difficult work at another post; it is one of the things that were involved in the system of apprenticeship, and also one of the things meant by the saying that "Freemasonry is a progressive science." Furthermore there is a more "human" angle to this fact that each office is a Station of, and to, itself; each office holder has learned this for himself if he has ever attempted to use the functions of another office. If a Junior Warden steps out of his Station to interfere in the Senior Warden's duties, there soon comes a moment when he discovers how bitter the latter's resentment can be. In theory it may at times be difficult to draw the exact line which separates the duties of one Station from another, but the officers on duty never have any difficulty in knowing where exactly that line is.

There are the offices: each one in its own place in the work and structure of the Lodge—the Master, the Wardens, and the Deacons; the Secretary and the Treasurer; the Tiler and the Stewards. Is it not true that each one has in it a certain air of greatness! There is no make-believe in any one of them; no hollow pretense; an incumbent does not busy himself with posturings or stupid formalities. What is done in them is done by men, with men, for men, and at those moments in men's lives when their manhood is most involved. For it would be difficult to say how important is the work done in a Lodge; and that is because what is done affects men in their character, their reputation, their sense of self-respect, their work, their fortunes and misfortunes, their fellowships and their friendships. The things required of a man who would hold one of these offices are more than perhaps he may have thought; there is therefore good reason to give thought to what means a man can employ to prepare himself for such a career in Masonry. I shall set down those means under six heads; and I shall put them in the form of directions to be followed, in order that you can have a clear course.

1. *Attend Lodge With Your Purpose in Mind.*

Tell certain of your Masonic friends who are in office, or
are in that kind of Lodge work, what your purpose is; nor
is there reason to shrink from doing so lest you be taken
to be too ambitious; tell them frankly, for they will be
glad to have you in their circle, knowing, as they do, that
there is always need to have new men in it. Once they
know your purpose, they will assist you to find a way into
those activities which go on in, or around, the various
Lodge offices. Attend Lodge regularly; and when in Lodge
take an active part in Lodge business, which is of itself
as much a form of "working," as is the conferring of Degrees. Join in the discussion of matters before the Lodge,
make or second motions, and if there be debate take part
in it; nor is it possible to learn Lodge business otherwise,
since no mere on-looker can have the "feel" of it, or know
its true inwardness in any other way.

If, in order to carry out what is decided upon in Lodge
business, committees are appointed, and you are tendered
an appointment, accept it, because there is no better way
to continue in Lodge work than to serve on Committees.
Why does a Lodge have committees? Because under its
form of organization there is no other means available to
carry on its work. What if it be decided to visit a Brother
in bed with illness? He is not there in the Lodge room and
therefore men must go to him, and the men who go are a
Committee. Or what if it be decided to have a Lodge
dinner? It cannot be cooked then and there; a Committee
must handle it. Yet, these, and a hundred things similar
to them, are what a Lodge does; and since this is so, when
committees do them that is the way in which the Lodge
does them—indeed, the idea of Lodge Committees may be
defined as "the Lodge working elsewhere." It may be that

in some societies or fraternities committee work has become a bugaboo because it is dull work and drudgery; you will have no such boredom to face in Lodge committees; on the contrary this work is frequently intensely interesting, exciting even, and a man may carry away from committee work some of the richest memories and experiences of his life.

Now it is not to be supposed that you would take part in Lodge business or in committee work merely to advance yourself toward your goal of holding Lodge office; that would be to act hypocritically, and probably defeat your own purpose. The point rather is that you would be engaged in those activities where you would find the practical knowledge of what offices are and what officers are required to do. While finding that knowledge you would have opportunities to ask information from the officers and past-officers with whom you would be in association; it is from them that such information can be best had, because they are the only men who have it. They are glad to give it, for each was once himself placed where you now stand.

2. *Be Willing to be Told*

If a man feels that to be told to do this or that thing in Lodge work means that he is "under" another, in the objectionable sense of that word, or that some officer is arbitrarily ordering him about to make a show of his authority, he is usually mistaken. In a Lodge it often occurs that some particular thing must be done, and a man must be "told off" to do it. That is the sole meaning of the word "told." What is an officer himself if not a man told off by the Lodge to be responsible for certain work, arduous work, and with responsibilities; how can he carry on his work without calling now and then for assistance?

There is something to be said beyond that, for if a man

raises the question of dignity, his question can be turned against him. Why is a man "told off"? It is because he is seen to possess some talent, ability, or other quality for a given task, so that it is a recognition that he receives, not an humiliation. This holds true even if what a man is told off to do may appear to be trivial or menial. Along with Lodge business in the large, and with committee business here and there, a number of small things come up to be done now and then which fall within the sphere of one of the offices. They are not trivial in themselves but they may appear to be, and in that very appearance is a trial or test for a man who, in his daily work, may have others, servants perhaps, to do such things for him. But what would you? Now and then there are errands to be run; there are costumes to be folded up and put away; there are such small offices to be performed as are incidental to the Preparation Room; once in awhile somebody must help with coffee and sandwiches or even wash dishes afterwards. There may be no obligation to volunteer to attend to those duties, but a man unwilling to be told off to do them is to that extent lacking in preparing himself to hold office. He who will not serve is not fit to command.

3. *Be Prepared to Substitute for Officers and Lodge Workers*

In some instances an officer is not allowed to have another man substitute for him, this being particularly true of the Worshipful Master; in other cases he is not allowed to have a substitute except it be another officer, and then only as the rules and regulations specify; but there are many places in the conferring of the Degrees where he can be substituted and the practice of doing so is common in many Lodges. You will find along this line one of the best possible schoolings; you should prepare yourself to take a part in the Ritual, not the whole of it at once, but beginning with one section of one Degree, and then going on to another part after that is mastered. Here again, it must be emphasized, you will be welcomed; few things contribute more to a busy Master's peace of mind than to have on the sidelines a Brother or two in readiness to take a part in conferring a Degree.

If you are now and then in a mood to remain home on the night of a Lodge communication, whether because it is raining or too cold or too hot, bear in mind that the Master, the Wardens, the Secretary also have their own moods. Why should not they remain at home? It is because they are officers. It belongs to their offices that they must be present. And that is one of the marks of a man who would be considered as a possible officer to be. When the members find that a man who has the purpose to prepare himself for office attends regularly, they know from that fact alone that he is sincere and dependable. From knowing this it is inevitably next in order that they will begin to count on him. And you also, if you find in yourself that steadiness of purpose, will know that you can count upon yourself.

If your regularity of attendance proves your steadfastness, for a similar reason it proves you to possess another qualification: that you have clear knowledge of the importance of the work of an officer. Suppose that on a night when a Degree is to be conferred one of the Wardens is at the last moment prevented from coming; what is to be done? Or that the Master, or the Secretary, is kept away? The work must go on. If in some instance you happen to be one who sees that it is carried on, it is *that* fact, not the mere fact that you are acting in place of another, which counts.

There is another fact at this point for you to consider.

The work a man does when he acts in an officer's place is not a substitute work but is the self-same work that the officer himself would have done. If you are to deliver a speech on a given occasion but are prevented from attending, and you have me deliver a speech in your place, the speech I shall deliver will be my own, and will therefore be a substitute for yours. But if an officer is prevented from taking his place in the conferring of a Degree and another acts for him, that other does not give some version of his own but gives the work word for word as the officer would have given it; there is nothing substituted. This fact rules out a certain feeling a man might have of being a make-shift, a stopgap; when you act for an officer you are, therefore, not preparing to do an officer's work in the future, but are doing it now. If you are doing it now then you have learned it; and if you have learned it then are you prepared, to that given extent, to hold that office, and that fact is established in the eyes of your Brethren.

4. *What About the Ritual?*

In such of your preparations as have mastery of the Ritual in view, it is a wise procedure to begin where the beginnings of such preparations are, by using two or three very simple methods. Keep at hand a good modern dictionary which gives the derivation of words as well as their pronunciations and definitions; and make it a point of honor never to let a word pass if you are not sure what it means or what is its correct pronunciation. And, if possible, have alongside it a copy of Dr. Albert G. Mackey's "Encyclopedia of Freemasonry," where, without further search, you have articles about all the symbols, ceremonies, and the duties of officers. He who knows the history, meaning and purpose of each portion or particular of a Degree; or of the Opening and Closing ceremonies, can understand what he is doing at any given moment but cannot otherwise know. There is no need for a Ritualist to be a scholar but there is need for him to make use of what the scholars have written.

To con the work, to learn it by heart, also comes down to certain definite methods. First, each Degree of itself divides into a number of units, each one with a beginning and an end, and it has a central point. If the student masters these one at a time, and one after another, he will find it much easier than to attempt to learn a Degree as a whole, all at once. After he has mastered a unit he will have more tenacious grasp of it than if he trusted to his general impressions. Second, rehearse each part privately, and over and over, going through it when alone as you would in Lodge; and, while doing so, be your own critic and audience in order to make sure that you enunciate the words distinctly and pronounce them so as to be heard. If a man cannot enact a portion of the Ritual when by himself, certainly he will be less able to do so with others present. Third, go now and then to study the work of competent Ritualists in your own Lodge, and also in other Lodges; and especially at each opportunity, when a Grand Lecturer, or a District Deputy is in your neighborhood, and listen to his instructions and comments.

The words "Ritual" and "Ritualist" themselves need to be clearly understood; and they have familiar uses elsewhere which are unlike our Masonic uses of them, and therefore confuse us if we do not have the Masonic uses thoroughly understood. In its broad general sense "ritual" means either that something is said in a fixed voice or something is done with a fixed movement, or else that certain formalities are observed to keep some meeting or assembly in order. In that sense there is some ritual in the Lodge but not much, and it is of no great importance.

It were better had we continued to employ the ancient designation, which was "work," and not only because it was the term generally employed until recent times but also because it better describes the nature of the Degrees and the Ceremonies. An officer conferring a Degree is not engaged in formalities or meaningless repetitions, but is at work, and the work has effects and results which are important and permanent. Nor does he "act" as in a play, that would be something to be witnessed by an audience; and we know that a candidate is not an audience, nor merely an auditor, but a participant, and, since so, is *himself* in what is being done. Still less does an officer "render" the work, which would be an unhappy task, since to render a spoken "part" would be to speak slowly here, rapidly there, with a low voice in one place, a high voice in another. Still less does he "recite" the Degrees, or any portion of them, like an elocutionist before a crowd. The most nearly correct of such words would be "enact," because it implies that an officer is himself in what he says and does, and yet even that word does not quite hit off the point.

It is best to think of one's self as a "worker," and of the Degrees as "work" because that most truly describes what is done. For consider what momentous consequences follow, once the officers have conferred a Degree! A man who until a short time ago was wholly outside the Fraternity, who was not only not permitted to enter the Lodge room but not even permitted to linger near its doors, is now *in* the Lodge, and is in it as a member. What he now, and henceforth, has in his mind and heart and by which his future may be reshaped, he did not have before. He is now entrusted to Masonry; but Masonry also entrusts itself to him, its work to his hands, its name and honor to his care. He has entered new ways of interest and activity, will form new friends and have new associates. Once the whole work of the Degrees is completed, he can thereafter take part in the business of the Lodge, vote, hold office; must pay over money to the treasurer; will have a voice in the use and expenditure of funds. Finally, he now stands under the laws of Masonry, which are not trivial and sometimes are formidable—as those know who have stood Masonic trial. In what sense can the means by which all this is effected be described as a mere formality? There were no greater nonsense than to describe it so: it is *work*, responsible work.

5. *Consult Your Friends.*

About what? It would not be of course to campaign for office, nor to ask for "backing," or for any such reasons whatever. That course would be fatal and unthinkable; a flagrant violation of Masonic Law and custom. Consult with them, engage in conversation with them, about your own aspirations and preparations; and about such affairs of the Lodge as belong to the officers and their work. For oftentimes from conversation a man can gain facts, knowledge, and understanding of some form of work that otherwise he could not obtain until he had himself engaged in it. You might have the feeling now and then that it would be more fitting to keep to yourself your aspirations; the feeling should be laid aside, and your friends would tell you to forget it, because they have that aspiration for you exactly as you have it for yourself. There has never been a secret made of the fact that there are some ten or so offices in a Lodge; that men must occupy them; that to work in one of them is not easy; and that whoever is willing to undertake such work will have a welcome beforehand from his Brethren.

Perhaps there will be among them a present officer, or

a past officer. When he discusses the work of an office it is not as when other men do; he has a knowledge of it that can be had only by occupying it, and in that are three sorts of particulars. For one thing, he knows what the office "feels like" from within, so that it is a far different sort of thing for him than what it "feels like" from without. For another, he knows what an officer must put up with, what he must face, and how it is to be "under fire," and what things are expected of him. And he knows at first hand what satisfaction a man has out of an office for himself.

There is an old tale told in the Bible that when a number of men sought to cross the fords in the Jordan they were stopped, and with considerable violence, because a word was required of them, but "they could not frame to pronounce it aright." What if you were to discover, out of your conversations with your Brethren, that the old parable may have certain applications to yourself? Perhaps a subtle delicacy in the discussion is called for here; or it may be, not; there is a possibility that any man may misread himself, so that, where he had considered himself qualified for a post, others are of a different mind. It will not be presumed that this can happen in your case. But suppose that it could, and what if it did? On that head one could bethink himself of at least two sage reflections. First, to take the worse ahead of the better, he could conclude like a philosopher that if, because of some trait of his personality, he would not be acceptable for a given post, it is best to know it beforehand instead of afterwards, lest he should have put himself to much preparation for nothing. Second, he could conclude like a theologian that if his lacks, or faults, are of the remediable sort he can set about to remedy them, and at once to qualify himself for office holding.

6. *Read.*

When in the 1840's Dr. Albert G. Mackey, a physician of wide practice in Charleston, S. C., and with a family to support and a large house to maintain, suddenly set his practice aside and began to prepare to write his "Encyclopedia of Freemasonry" and his "History of Freemasonry," his friends were dumfounded. Why this break away from his practice? Why throw aside a public career? But he knew what he was about. In after years he gave an explanation, and the substance of it was that the time had come when Freemasonry could no longer go forward without books. He said that in the olden days, not only the secret work but also the history, traditions, laws, teachings, and the interpretation of the symbols had been carried on by word of mouth. But that, he went on, was because Lodges then were scattered and were small; Masonic activities were few and simple; and not much was known of the history and practices of the Craft. But now a new condition had arisen. Lodges were multiplying, and growing larger. They were establishing themselves in every community, and their influence, making itself felt, had begun to bring them under scrutiny by the public. Moreover there were more laws, and yet more to come; and, now that competent scholars were devoting themselves to it, Masonic history was growing to mountainous proportions. There was need to have this mass of knowledge brought into order, and arranged, and put into books, so that each Mason could have it in a manageable form. And he predicted that what was true then would become more true in the future. His prediction has been fulfilled. It is more necessary than ever before for a Mason to read because the Craft has grown so large, and its activities are so complex.

1. At this point consider a Lodge as a structure, with

certain parts, and each part designed to fit in at a certain place, and to have a certain purpose. Consider that the offices belong to that structure, and that each office has a structure of its own. Then take it that this structure as a whole is what a Lodge is in the eyes of Masonic law. What there is for a Masonic officer in this is, of course, that he must not expect that his office can ever be altered from what the law defines it to be, and that what he as an officer does must be in conformity with it. It is not that a man preparing himself to quality for an office must read the whole body of Masonic law, but it is wise for you to read carefully what in the law applies to the offices. You can find that in these and in similar books: The Book of Constitutions or Masonic Code of your own Grand Lodge; any Commentary that your Grand Lodge may have published on its own Laws; the By-Laws of your Lodge and there are general works on Masonic law in which are pages or chapters on the same themes, as: "Masonic Jurisprudence," by A. G. Mackey; "Lectures on Masonic Jurisprudence," by Roscoe Pound, and there are a number of scattered articles in Mackey's "Encyclopedia."

2. The second group has for its point what the offices are in the work, what are the rights, duties, prerogatives of officers, and so on forth. Unfortunately there have as yet been few books written for this particular purpose, and that fact is the Craft's misfortune. Excellent for this purpose, is "Our Stations and Places," by Henry G. Meacham. Brother Meacham has written his book out of an abundant experience; for many years he has made of the office of Grand Lecturer a profession, and he has had need to do so, because he must inspect each year more than one thousand Lodges, and shepherd the work of half a hundred District Lecturers.

3. The purpose of this last group is to know the history

xplanations of the symbols,
h are connected with them;
east a number of them, will
g knowledge of the duties
ond, will increase, expand
them. Under the head of
nasonry," by Melvin M.
ize as this one. A classic
F. Gould—this is a hard,
masterpiece. Under the
: "Symbolism of Free-
mbolical Masonry," by

s
h
m
H

Under the most favorable circumstances Masonic books
are sometimes difficult to come by, but if you will carry
out the injunction "seek and you shall find" you will find
that injunction to be true. If a book is still in print it can
be purchased from, or through, book-stores or publishers.
If not, it usually can be found second-hand through local
book-stores with facilities for advertising among second-
hand dealers. You may be able to borrow a book from a
Masonic friend; or from a public library, many of which
have Masonic books on their shelves; or from your own
Lodge, if it have a library (as it should), or from a neighboring Lodge's Library; or from some Grand Lodge Library with circulation privileges. If your Grand Lodge has
an Educational Committee you can make inquiries of it.
If any book recommended above is not to be had, then
you may find another one as good, or with something good
in it. But it is best to read no books whatever unless they
are "duly and truly prepared, worthy and well qualified"—
and intelligent: Books that are too old, or far-fetched, or
freakish, or ride a hobby, or are propaganda for some cult
or parasitic "movement" are worse than nothing.

You have had in those six directions the methods by which a man can prepare himself for Lodge office. They have been of a nature which shows what work there is not only in preparing for office, but in discharging the duties of the offices themselves. If they have at times stressed what a man must take to the office, they have also not infrequently showed what the office gives to the man. But there is not any reward held out to an officer, and no wages paid; and every Freemason knows why it is so. However, in another sense, the reward is great; and what it is, and in what form, it is next in order for us to discuss. It may not be in one sense a sufficient reward, because a man must devote so much of himself, his energies, his money, his time; but it is in another sense an invaluable reward, because it is, in itself, beyond any means to evaluate it. There are five heads under which we shall describe it.

1. *Etiquette.*

The word "etiquette" is from the French language, and meant originally "a la carte"; that is, "according to written instructions." At receptions in the great houses, where men and women of high rank in Paris society were entertained, the guests were received according to rank and title, those of more distinguished position being ushered into the reception room ahead of those of lesser rank. To save him any embarrassment a guest was given a written card to show him his place in the line. There was nothing artificial in that usage of etiquette; it was in the spirit and purpose of politeness and good manners, which are always the same. Here in our American society, where we have no ranks and titles, we have the same etiquette; there are such occasions as guests to be received at the door, distinguished visitors in the community to be introduced; in our private circles women go through a door ahead of the men, the young give precedence to their elders, strangers are welcomed with politeness to make them feel at home; and in each instance there is a recognized and established form of doing so.

In Freemasonry we have a complete code of etiquette which comprehends every officer and member in it. Each Grand Officer is in a rank and has a title. When the Grand Master enters the Grand Lodge room he has a fixed place in the procession of his officers; when he takes his place in the Grand East he is conducted there according to a fixed form and receives a salute in recognition of his rank. And in the mode of etiquette which belongs to his Station are provided the forms in which the other Grand Officers go according to rank and are conducted to their Stations or places. In the majority of Grand Lodges throughout the world a Grand Master has on his personal staff a Grand Officer, usually named the Grand Marshall, to make sure that etiquette is unbroken in assemblies of the Grand Lodge, and that the proper forms are observed wherever the Grand Master may go on official visits throughout the year.

In the constituent Lodge the Worshipful Master has a corresponding duty to make sure that etiquette is observed among his own members. He has forms for receiving visiting Grand Officers to his Lodge, and other modes for admitting visiting officers and members from other Lodges. He himself goes and comes, in the Lodge room or in procession outside it, according to his rank, and is saluted or addressed according to his title. His officers also have their own ranks and grades, which have been established in the Craft for centuries, and each one with usages of etiquette appropriate to it.

Thus for a man working in it, Freemasonry is a school of etiquette; perhaps there is nowhere a greater or a more perfect one, or one where there are so large a number and variety of the forms and usages which politeness and good manners call for. And if a man is in one of the offices he is working where the use of etiquette is most continuous. If therefore you are considering what it would mean to you to devote six or seven years to Lodge office you can be in certainty of this, that you would have permanently for yourself a facility and mastery of the ways of etiquette.

2. *Deportment.*

Deportment is a man's manner of behavior when in an assembly. If when a man is in any one assembly he sees why a given manner of behavior is in order there, he has seen what deportment is in any other kind of assembly. There are in it two modes of behavior. One of them is a mode of speaking and of moving about, which has for its purposes not to disturb others or to interrupt what is being said and done. The other is a man's mode of sitting, of standing, of mien, of carriage, of dignity, and it is determined by the purpose not to attract attention to himself. An assembly of Masons in Lodge has its own particular form of decorum, but the deportment which is in order in it is identical with deportment anywhere else.

When a man is in an office, while in an assembly of Brethren, his own manner of behavior has a larger importance than it could have if he were sitting in the sidelines; it has it for four reasons. (1) He acts and speaks as an officer and must therefore comport himself in a manner appropriate to his position. (2) He remains in his own place throughout, and therefore cannot shift to another part of the room, or leave the assembly, as a Brother on the sidelines might do, and could do, without violating decorum. (3) He is in plain view of the assembly, on a platform, or else out in front of the others, and he accordingly has more reason to take care not to disturb, or to attract attention to himself. (4) There are periods of time when he is not active at his post; he will at such times not converse in whispers with Brothers near him, or gesture or motion to men across the room, or sit ungracefully. He will always keep his knees together and both feet on the floor.

If a man were working in Lodge office evening after evening, year after year, he would be singularly unimpressionable if he were to remain unaffected in himself by his continual attention to deportment. You would in time acquire an instinctive sense of the manner of behavior in order at any occasion, anywhere; and that would mean a freedom from embarrassment, and a lack of awkwardness, and a spontaneous sense of dignity.

3. *Executive and Administrative Ability.*

Before a man enters an office he has some knowledge of it, but there is seldom a man who, once he is in it, does not find more work to do than he had expected, and of more various kinds. Some of the officers have a larger number of duties than the others; the Wardens do, for example, the Secretary, and the Treasurer; but the office of Worshipful Master, in this respect as in so many others, is in a class apart, for it has at one stroke the duties belonging to itself and the responsibility to supervise the other offices. If a man were curious to discover for himself how many and how diverse are those duties, and were to analyze them with technical care, he would find them divided into no fewer than twelve heads or classes. The Master presides over his Lodge. He represents it in the Grand Lodge. He directs, or instructs, and is responsible for the other officers. He appoints the members of standing and special committees, with few exceptions, and may sit with them or have a part in their work. He signs the minutes, counter-signs checks, has correspondence to read and write. He is in charge of the conferring of each Degree, and has the largest part in each one. He sees that the sick are visited, that those in need of relief are cared for, and that the Lodge when called upon shall perform its duties at funerals and interments. The maintenance and care of the Lodge room, or the Lodge building, is delegated to others, but it is his responsibility to see that they do not fail in their duties. If the Lodge appears in public he leads it, and may speak for it. He has duties of a legal and disciplinary kind. He must maintain peace and harmony. He receives and entertains visiting Lodge and Grand Lodge officers. Meanwhile he has relations with his members personally and privately, and there may be times when this will take more out of his head, and his heart, than any other calls made upon him.

What does a man bring away from a year spent in such an office? He has been an executive. He has had an experience with laws, regulations, rules. He has been an administrator. He has presided over assemblies, and has become familiar with the Masonic form of parliamentary law. He has learned to speak in public. And he has had, and not only in his year as Worshipful Master but for many years, an abundant experience of being among men, of leading them, and of dealing with them. These qualities, abilities, and knowledge, once his term in the highest of the Lodge offices is finished, he has for himself, and will have ever. They are not to be lightly appraised, because in themselves they are among the abilities and qualities most highly valued anywhere.

4. *Language.*

You have learned already how much you must do in order to learn the words of the Ritual; it is now in order for you to consider what they would mean to you after you had completed it. In the Degrees and Ceremonies which a man must learn by heart, and for years continue to have by heart, there are so many words, phrases and sentences that if they could be written down they would fill a large book. There is that largeness in it; there is also a great diversity in it, for it is drawn from the vocabularies of many arts, trades, professions, from history, and from the Bible. There are in it the words of prose, of poetry, of prayer, of narration, of oratory, of the drama. That language has come to us out of many periods and countries; here and there are phrases which have come from ancient times. It is full of the speech of the Middle Ages. Its dramatic passages were shaped in the Renaissance, its monitorial portions were from the Enlightenment, there are Hebrew words in it, phrases out of the Greek, sonorous sentences which came from the Latin, words and phrases from the Saxon, from Early English and from Middle English. And it is of a quality, as was said above, that is found only in the great masterpieces of literature.

A man would be rewarded if he were to read in a book that much language, and of that quality; but it might not remain with him. Perhaps, if he were to learn it by heart, he would be more richly rewarded, but even then he could not retain it long because it is only by continual use that words stay in the memory. There is only one means to possess language permanently, and a man has that means in the work of the Ritual. It is to make actual use of it, and to employ it in actual use over and over. The words then become a part of himself; and if, in the beginning, a man were to say to himself, "This language is not mine, it belongs to the Ritual," at the end he could say, "This language belongs to the Ritual, and it also belongs to me. It is in my blood and bones, and will remain in me as long as I live."

It is not as if you were to put yourself to school. But
what if you did? Would not such a schooling be worth
having? How do men elsewhere come by their command
of words, their free and flowing speech, their unstudied
ease in expressing, in telling, in expounding, in narrating?
They were not born with the golden spoon of eloquence
in their mouths; nor did they perfect their accomplish-
ment between breakfast and dinner! They put themselves
to school somewhere, such a school as you would have in
mastering the Three Degrees.

5. *The Greatness of the Ritual.*

When you are beginning your preparation for office you
will become interested in the Ritual as a thing to learn,
and in your efforts to master it; after you have been conferring Degrees for a year or two you will find yourself
becoming interested in it for its own sake. The Ritual is
vast in itself; a man can enter it, and can move about in it,
ever discovering new realms within it, and find it growing
more interesting with each step he takes. That is especially
true for an officer who is working in it, because for him
it ceases to be as something seen from without; he is enacting it, has himself in it, and he comes to know it as it
is from within.

There is never any telling what it may set him to thinking about. It may be about geometry; or the Operative
Masons in a cathedral; or about music; his thoughts may
be in Jerusalem; or he may be thinking about what it is
to die; or who, and what, were the men who had the
Liberal Arts and Sciences for their schooling; or how there
came to be in the world this thing or that thing, or another,
as the symbols and emblems one after another remind him
of them. Scholars are by profession men of learning; they
have many things and great things ever in their minds;

but there has scarcely been a Masonic scholar yet who has not confessed what surprise he felt when he discovered how large a world is in the Ritual, how multifarious that world is, how many paths and gates there are in it, leading away into far-off fields of knowledge, and countries of the mind.

What is it that has kept men working in it these many centuries? Why do they not weary of it? Because there is in it a secret which is its own, namely: it tells little rather than much, but the little it tells leads a man to find out much for himself. If in its beginnings in the Middle Ages it had consisted of a set of lectures, expounding and discussing abstract subjects, it would be as dead now as are the other lectures of the Middle Ages. But that is not its way, and it nowhere else is Freemasonry's way; rather its way is to embody some truth or idea in a symbol, a ceremony, a rite, a picture, to set it thus in a man's mind without comment, and then to leave it there for him to think about, and to ponder, and to return to. It never does his thinking for him, but it has a thousand arts to make him think for himself. You will find out that secret for yourself as time goes on; and one of the rewards you will have for mastering the Ritual, and for working in it year after year, will be to discover, after a time, that you have the whole of it in your mind for the rest of your days—not as a set of words and phrases, but as living thoughts.

We began by saying that if you had an aspiration to find in Lodge office your own form of Masonic work and experience, you should let your aspiration be known; we have ended by endeavoring to show what would be the reward for yourself were you to devote yourself to the offices for six or seven years. Our discussion has now drawn a full circle because it has returned to the point from which it departed in the beginning.

CHAPTER II

LODGE AND GRAND LODGE OFFICES

IN A COUNTRY which has no Grand Lodge of its own, and is therefore described in the nomenclature of Masonic jurisprudence as "open country," any regular Grand Lodge anywhere, on the other side of the world it may be, may issue to a group of Master Masons, who petition for it, a charter to form a Lodge; this charter may be called by any one of several names, "deputation," "warrant," "constitution," etc., but if it is signed by the executive officers and carries the seal of a Regular Grand Lodge it contains in itself sufficient authority to make a Lodge when the petitioners for it have complied with the provisions of it. Other Grand Lodges, in other parts of the world, may similarly constitute new Lodges in that same "open country"—"open" in the Masonic sense, not in the sense of being unpopulated; or, as it may chance, other Lodges may be chartered by the same Grand Lodge as the first one.

After a sufficient number of Lodges have been thus constituted and have, by the passage of time proved themselves to be permanently established—three or more of them, their Grand Lodges consenting usually (though not necessarily always) may unite in a convention held under the usages of accepted Masonic parliamentary law and, of themselves, may form a new Grand Lodge. Once this new Grand Lodge is established, its constituent Lodges surrender to it their old charters and receive new ones in place of them, their names and numbers henceforth being such as are specified in the new charters. This new Grand Lodge will then proclaim itself the exclusive and sovereign Masonic authority over a given territory, which is called its Grand Jurisdiction; this Grand Jurisdiction may or may not coincide with the political boundary of a state or some political territory or subdivision of a state, but usually it will. If, as may possibly occur, it is to share jurisdiction with another Grand Lodge, then it has concurrent Grand Jurisdiction; but, if so, it is the practice for the sharing Grand Lodges to agree among themselves; but even in concurrent jurisdictions the Grand Lodge has absolute undivided authority over its own Lodges, they in turn having their own local jurisdiction, and in such a case the Lodges and their local jurisdictions together comprise that Grand Lodge's Grand Jurisdiction.

A new Grand Lodge will wish to share in what is called the "comity" of Grand Lodges, which is world-wide. This means that while a given Grand Lodge is absolutely sovereign over its own Grand Jurisdiction, brooking no interference from without and suffering none of its constituent Lodges to give it a divided allegiance or a qualified obedience, it may by its own action be in fraternal relationship with other Grand Lodges, exchanging courtesies and correspondence, visiting back and forth, conferring courtesy degrees; it may be, and, as we do here in the United States, exchanging Grand Lodge representatives who may visit in a Grand Communication, be introduced there, and have the courtesies of the floor, but are not permitted to vote. The means by which a new Grand Lodge enters this "comity" or voluntary fellowship of other Grand Lodges is by "Recognition"; the new Grand Lodge corresponds with one or more other Grand Lodges already established, in so doing it asks for Recognition and at the same time produces evidence of its own regularity, whereupon, usually on motion by a Grand Committee, the second Grand Lodge votes upon it. Henceforth in the eyes of the Grand Lodges thus recognizing it, the new Grand Lodge is regular, and members of the Lodges in each of them may visit or demit back and forth. For obvious reasons each Grand Lodge desires to be thus recognized by as many other regular Grand Lodges as possible; and since this is so, a general, world-wide comity is evermore extending itself. At the present time no one Grand Lodge recognizes each and every other Grand Lodge, sometimes because recognition has not been sought and sometimes because regularity is questioned, but the tendency everywhere is for Grand Lodges to extend comity as universally and as rapidly as possible. The day may come in the distant future when there will be as many Grand Lodges as the world will need; when each populated country will be in an exclusive Grand Jurisdiction; and when each and every Grand Lodge will have recognized every other one; when that day comes, though not until it does come, will Freemasonry be world-wide in actual fact as well as universal in spirit and potentiality.

It may occur that when a new Lodge is constituted in an "open country" it will be in some sense irregular; it may have a flaw in its charter, or may fail to conform to a charter's provisions, or in its activity may violate one of the Ancient Landmarks, or among its members, one or two may not have been regularly made; everything of this sort is "healed" or "regularized" the moment it receives its new charter from the Grand Lodge in which it becomes a constituent. It may be that a new Grand Lodge may also find itself to be in some detail similarly irregular, perhaps through inadvertence or because of the action taken by a misguided minority; if so, it will discover the fact when it comes to ask for Recognition from other Grand Lodges; in that event it can act to regularize itself or to heal itself, and the receiving of Recognition from other regular Grand Lodges is a sign to the Masonic world that it has done so.

Freemasonry is not propagated by official acts and documents; it is self-propagated. That is, a few individual Masons from various sources find their way into a community in an "open country" without a Lodge; through their private, voluntary action they petition some Grand Lodge of their choice, and, until they can be in a Grand Lodge of their own, must do the best they can in their local Lodge and with possibly very little supervision from a distance; under such circumstances it is inevitable that there shall be mistakes made and that a certain amount of irregularity may ensue; this is understood, and therefore such a Lodge and its members are regularized when they receive a new charter from their own new Grand Lodge, "regularizing" after the event is one of the cornerstones. This regular and recognized custom of "healing" and of Masonic Jurisprudence and is there known as the "de facto" principle. This is in contrast to the "de jure" principle usually in practice elsewhere in accordance with which an organization begins with an official, written document, and is irregular if there is a flaw in that document; and continues to be as long as the document is in force. This distinction is important to know because only confusion can result where a "de facto" system is treated as if it were a "de jure" one.

If it be true, as it was presupposed in the preceding chapter, that you have a reasonable hope of occupying an office in a Lodge, and a Lodge here in the United States, your own Lodge is a constituent member of a Grand Lodge. There are forty-nine Grand Lodges in the United States, each one having a State for its Grand Jurisdiction, excepting in the case of the Grand Lodge of the District of Columbia. Comity in the United States is complete, each one recognizing each and every other Grand Lodge; because of this you are eligible to visit in any of the 16,000, or so, Lodges or may demit to any one of them. A few of these Grand Lodges have Lodges outside our national boundaries, in the Canal Zone, in example, in Alaska, and Japan, etc., but in all likelihood the Lodges in your Grand Lodge will all be within your State boundaries. When, therefore, you go from one State to another you are never outside the American system of Masonry; if however you travel abroad, into Mexico, or South America, or in Europe, you can visit in only such Lodges as are under Grand Lodges that are recognized by your own Grand Lodge.

Your Grand Lodge itself works under a body of Masonic law which is binding both on itself and on its constituent Lodges; this law is for purposes of study and description, though not in respect of its authority divided under two heads: the Unwritten, and the Written. There has ever been in Freemasonry a continuing body of traditions, customs, rules, regulations, and principles which are as a whole comparable to the common law in the system of civil law; they are binding because they belong to the essence of Freemasonry or else are customary; they may be written or declared by Grand Lodges but cannot be exhaustively or finally defined by any form of words, and neither gain nor lose in authority by virtue of being written or unwritten. This is about the Unwritten Law. At the center of this body of Unwritten Law are the Ancient Landmarks. Some Grand Lodges have written these down and made lists of them; others have never done so; it matters nothing one way or another because the Landmarks do not gain anything by being written nor are they made ambiguous by the fact that written lists of them vary in number. A Landmark is something which belongs to what Freemasonry is, and in such a way that if it were destroyed, Freemasonry would be destroyed along with it. Each Grand Lodge works *under* the Landmarks; no Grand Lodge is superior to them; if a Grand Lodge were to take such an action as would destroy a Landmark, that action would be an Innovation; if it were to become guilty of an Innovation other regular Grand Lodges would withdraw their Recognition of it—it would be outlawed and every Lodge in it would become a clandestine Lodge.

Based on the common laws and the Landmarks of the Craft is the Book of Constitutions, which is the cornerstone of the Written Law, and of which the prototype was that Book of Constitution which the Mother Grand Lodge adopted in 1723. Along with this are a number of statutes (called by various names) which a Grand Lodge adopts for itself, and which are fundamental to its work in its own Grand Jurisdiction, but which do not hold for other Grand Lodges, each of which has its own. In addition are a number of written regulations, rules, edicts, and opinions, each of which is the law within its own special sphere, and possessing among themselves varying degrees of authority. In American Grand Jurisdictions these written and established laws and rules are gathered together and printed in a single volume, which may be entitled the "Book of Constitutions," or "The Constitution," or "The Code," etc. If you are preparing yourself to hold Lodge office your own Grand Lodge Code is a volume important for you to read, study and have ever at hand.

When the first, or Mother, Grand Lodge was erected in

London in 1717 it was described as "Grand" in the sense
of "great, large, inclusive," and it was designed to be a
Lodge of which the members would be Lodges, thereby
paralleling the Lodge of which the members are individual
Masons. It was in the beginning *constituted* by four Lodges
—it was a union of Lodges, which union at the same time
had authority over the member Lodges. For this reason
Lodges have ever since been called "constituent Lodges";
they are often loosely described as "local," or "particular,"
or "subordinate," but none of these terms is accurate. For
centuries before 1717 many hundreds of Lodges existed independently, with no Grand Lodge, by Time Immemorial
rights and powers; certain of those Time Immemorial
rights were surrendered to the Grand Lodge after 1717
A.D. but ever so many of them remain; hence a Lodge is
not a *creature* of a Grand Lodge but has inherent in itself
a set of rights and powers which no Grand Lodge could
take away from it. The quality of being constituent therefore lies in the very nature of Freemasonry and is itself an
Ancient Landmark. A Lodge, however, is constituent of its
Grand Lodge only and cannot divide its allegiance either
with another Grand Lodge or with a Grand Body in one
of the High Grades; in every Regular Grand Jurisdiction
in the world the first Three Degrees are under Grand
Lodge authority, and are so exclusively.

The membership of a Grand Lodge consists of its Grand
officers and of delegates from each of its constituent
Lodges, which delegates usually are the Worshipful Masters, though in some Grand Jurisdictions both the Master
and the Wardens sit in Grand Lodge. When a Grand
Lodge meets, and is opened in due form, it is said to be
in Grand Communication. A Grand Communication may
be Emergent (or Special, or Called—nomenclature varies),
as in such cases when a Grand Lodge is convened for a

Grand Lodge funeral, a dedication, consecration of a temple, reception of a distinguished guest, and so on forth; or it may be a Regular or Stated Grand Communication. In a few instances in America these Regular Grand Communications are held at frequent stated times (stated in their Code) even four times a year, but in the majority of instances they are held once a year and may be held in the same place each year, or in places chosen a year in advance. While in Regular Grand Communication, a Grand Lodge follows an order of Business which usually consists of Opening Ceremonies, Calling of Roll, Reading of Minutes, an Address by the Grand Master, Reports of Committees, old and new Business, Introductions of distinguished guests, Election and Installation of Officers, and Ceremonies of Closing; and in most instances lasts over a period of two or three days. Within a short time after a Regular Grand Communication the Grand Secretary publishes and distributes in book form to the Lodges and Grand Officers a volume called "The Proceedings" in which are printed the Transactions of the Grand Communication accompanied by Tables of Statistics and lists of Lodges, and an Appendix usually called "The Fraternal Correspondence Report," which consists of an extensive review of the Proceedings of the other Grand Jurisdictions with which the Grand Lodge is in fraternal relations. This volume is also one which you, as a prospective Lodge officer, should be familiar with and keep at hand along with the Grand Lodge Code for study and reference, for while the majority of the duties of a Lodge officer concern the internal affairs of the Lodge only, a certain number of them have reference to the Grand Lodge. The work of the Lodge faces two ways: one, toward its own members and in its local jurisdiction; the other, toward the Grand Lodge and toward other Lodges.

It is at this point of contact between a Grand Lodge and its Lodges that many of the difficulties and complexities of Masonic Jurisprudence most clearly emerge. This subject of Jurisprudence is too large to be discussed in any one book, even in broadest outline, but there are certain facts about it which may be easily grasped; and it is just here in this present connection perhaps that those facts will be most helpful. Our statement of them will be informal, not in technical terms, and they will be chosen for their usefulness for our present purpose: 1. At every point Masonic Jurisprudence differs from the laws, rules, and forms of organization of other societies, more particularly from civil jurisprudence, and not only in details of form and practice, but also in fundamental principles—to lose sight of this fact, even for a moment, throws a student of Freemasonry into confusion. 2. There has been a body of practice and tradition from the origin of Freemasonry to the present; it has to some extent modified and changed itself but in essentials has remained the same, and its continuity has never been broken; the powers and authorities and duties of Lodges, Grand Lodges, and their Officers inhere in that fundamental, underlying, traditional body of Freemasonry—a fact expressed in the doctrine of the Ancient Landmarks, none of which can be contravened by any Lodge or Grand Lodge. 3. Because this is true it is said in the language of our Jurisprudence that the majority of the powers and rights of Grand Lodges, Lodges, Officers, and Members are "inherent"—that is, they have never been ordained, or devised, or commanded by any Body of Masons but belong to this essence of what Freemasonry is. 4. One facet of this fact is expressed by saying that a Lodge is a "constituent" of Grand Lodge and not its creature or subordinate; for the Freemasonry in a Lodge is traditional, originated before Grand

Lodges, is not created by a Grand Lodge but is inherent in a Lodge; much of the supervision, therefore, which a Grand Lodge wields over its Lodges is not to force the Lodges to carry out orders from the Grand Lodge (though it may be that) but rather it is to make sure that no Lodge fails to use the powers inherent in it and does not violate the Ancient Landmarks; expressed otherwise; a Grand Lodge has no power over certain things in a Lodge or a Lodge office.

5. It is for the same reason a mistake to suppose that the sole function of a Grand Lodge is to exercise its superior authority *over* a Lodge—as if it existed merely to exhibit a Lodge's subordination or its own powers of discipline. A Grand Lodge is also the *servant* of its own Lodges; they can use it as much as it can use them. For a Lodge to be jealous of a Grand Lodge's authority or to be suspicious of Grand Lodge officers is evidence of a mistaken view of the relationship between them, and argues a failure of knowledge. 6. Freemasonry as a whole, the single, indivisible Fraternity, is the ultimate unit and ground of authority; the Masonic system is its means to carry on its own work; and Lodges and Grand Lodges together, and at the same time, exist for its sake; there cannot be any conflict between the two, no jealousy, and no arbitrary lines of division. 7. The individual Mason, also, is, as it were, an institution in the Fraternity; he has a title, which is "Brother"; and certain inherent powers, rights, and privileges which neither Lodges nor Grand Lodges can (or ever would wish) to take away from him.

8. The ultimate units in the organized Masonic system, and therefore of Masonic Jurisprudence are: the Grand Lodge; the office of Grand Master; the constituent Lodge; the office of Worshipful Master; and the individual member. But it is often impossible to say where one of these

leaves off and the other begins; just as a line cannot be drawn between any two adjoining colors in the spectrum because one gradually merges into the other, so is it difficult to draw a hard-and-fast line between the adjacent institutions in Masonic Jurisprudence. What, for example, is one to do when a question appears to raise the problem as to the exact point where the authority of the Grand Lodge leaves off, and the authority of a Lodge begins? From its origin Freemasonry has ever left such questions to be decided on the spot by the knowledge and intelligence of Masons, rather than to attempt to fix a hard and rigid line by a written document. Documents, printed constitutions and rules, these have their own large and necessary place; but they are never complete enough to dispense with Masons' knowledge and understanding of Freemasonry as a whole, so that to gain for himself that comprehensive understanding must be the ultimate goal of each man who seeks to prepare himself for Masonic office. 9. Finally, and by token of the same facts, any principle or rule or fundamental practice is likely to have, as it were, more than one side or face. Thus, to offer one case out of a hundred, consider the Worshipful Master; he is executive head of his Lodge, and there is no appeal from his decisions; and yet a member has inherent rights which no Master can take away from him; and yet, again, he is subordinate to the Grand Master; and yet, still again, he has in his office inherent powers which a Grand Master cannot contravene. It is usually misleading to make any absolute, final statement about any office, practice, or principle, because the facts, if pushed on around to another side of the subject, oftentimes present a different face, and this, to repeat, leads once again to that which is the ultimate need; to have a complete knowledge, a general grasp, an understanding of Freemasonry as a whole is the first requirement; once that is in your possession, you will have little difficulty with the facts and problems of Lodges and Grand Lodges, of Lodge and Grand Lodge officers.

A Grand Lodge has legislative powers for its Grand Jurisdiction; is the court of final jurisdiction in the enforcement of the laws; has supreme executive and administrative powers. It issues and revokes Lodge charters. In matters of general comity and in inter-Grand Jurisdictional matters it and it alone can speak and act for its Grand Jurisdiction. When it requires the use of funds it supplies them out of dues levied through the Lodge on each member; out of fees, as when it receives a portion of initiation fees to use for special purposes; out of assessments made for extraordinary purposes; out of voluntary funds raised among craftsmen at its request for such extraordinary purposes as War Relief; and from gifts and from the interest on endowments. Grand Lodges, with almost no exceptions, support and administer general charities; Masonic homes and hospitals, and for these find the money by setting aside a portion of dues received and from gifts, endowments, and assessments. Many of them own their own Temples, in which they have a Grand Lodge auditorium and permanent headquarters for its offices; and a number of them support and maintain such services as Grand Lodge Libraries, Museums, and employment services. In addition to these fixed and regular organizational activities and functions, a Grand Lodge also is a general source of information for its whole Grand Jurisdiction; assists and helps Lodges and Lodge officers in a number of ways not made obligatory by the laws; and is at the same time the origin of general activities; services, and "movements" by which the whole Craft is benefitted.

While it may meet in executive and legislative Grand Communications only once a year, in reality a Grand

Lodge never sleeps, but is on duty without cessation day and night every day of the year; and while its offices and Communications are held in a specified place it is in reality present everywhere in its Grand Jurisdiction, and, in fact, wherever a member of one of its own Lodges may be, even though it may be in a foreign country; in effect it is the whole body of Masons in a given Grand Jurisdiction's organized and working together for their common good and welfare and to the end that Freemasonry, as it lies under its care, may be protected against disharmony from within or invasion from without and kept in health and made prosperous. Its scheme of organization may on paper be as dry and as colorless as a geometric diagram; its printed laws may be as hard to read as a table of statistics; its business sessions may be, to an outsider, long and heavy; but they who work in it year after year find it to be active and alive, warm, fruitful, filled with passion and compassion, interesting always and sometimes exciting, so that busy men work in it and for it, through many days of labor without pay and often at an expense defrayed out of their own pockets. It is a wonderful organization with which no man can think of another to compare it, and the work done in it is so self-rewarding that at the end men declare the labor and cost they have given to it "as dust in the balance."

The number and names of Grand offices differ a little from one American Grand Jurisdiction to another but there will be in each one a small number which are elective, and a much larger number which are appointive by the Grand Master. The elective offices usually are Grand Master, Deputy Grand Master, Senior Grand Warden, Junior Grand Warden, Grand Secretary and Grand Treasurer. Grand Lodge Committees are Permanent, or Constitutional, provided for in the written Grand Lodge Code;

or Special. A Special Committee may be created for a particular purpose by a Grand Communication or it may be created by the Grand Master; in nearly all instances Committee Members of both sorts are appointed by the Grand Master, and usually for one year though there are a few committees here and there among the Grand Jurisdictions on which an appointment is for a term of years, or may even be permanent. A Grand Master may also appoint what may be described as a temporary committee for some purpose of a purely local kind and lasting but a day or two. A Permanent (or Standing, or Constitutional) Committee may be in charge of a work of very great importance and be responsible for large sums of money; their Reports as published in Grand Lodge Proceedings oftentimes are invaluable documents in which, if a man studies them, he will learn much about Grand Lodge theory and practice; this holds true especially of the published Report of the Committee on Fraternal Correspondence (as it oftenest is called) which is a composite portrait of the activities of the whole American Craft year by year. The work done by Grand Committees of each and every sort, taking them as a whole and including the Grand Jurisdiction generally, tends to fall into two classes; first, those that carry out detailed instructions laid down by the printed Code, or by Grand Lodge action in Grand Communication, or by the Grand Master; second, those entrusted to carry out some general purpose, the detailed means and methods being left to the Committee itself.

A Grand Lodge is the custodian of the Ritual in its Jurisdiction. There is seldom any need for the Ritual to be discussed in Grand Jurisdictions because questions do not arise and for that reason the subject does not at first sight appear to loom large in Grand Lodge activities; but on a long range view of it the custodianship of the Ritual is very probably its most important single responsibility. The Ritual was transmitted to us by word of mouth from days long before the erection of the first Grand Lodge in 1717. After that Grand Lodge Period of 1717–1740 a number of "versions" were in use, and it was left to each Lodge to choose its own version. But this did not prove satisfactory in America because it resulted in too much confusion and led to too many abuses; there came to be too great a difference between the versions, too many irresponsible changes were made, and there grew up a class of "Ritual Mongers" or "Degree Pedlars" who went about selling versions for a fee, and the result was that a way was opened for each Lodge to have a Ritual of its own, and even to have a new one each year. About a century ago the Grand Lodges put an end to these multiplying divergences, adopted each one a Uniform Version for itself, and by enactment of law, compelled each and every Lodge to employ the same Version and provided means to supervise the Ritual continually. To carry out this custodianship and supervision a Grand Lodge may employ any one of various established methods; it may have one Grand Lodge officer charged with that duty, called by some such name as Grand Lecturer, and assisted by a staff appointed by himself; or it may have a Committee or Board instead of a single officer; or one of the Grand Officers may have custodianship of the Ritual as one of his several duties; and in addition there may be a system of local, or district, supervisors or lecturers. Regardless of what methods may be employed the purpose everywhere is the same, to make sure that the Ritual among the Lodges is kept uniform, and that no innovations creep in from year to year.

Within its own limits, and in the sphere proper to it, a Constituent Lodge is co-equal to a Grand Lodge, has an equal sovereignty with time immemorial rights, and these rights are imprescriptible and inalienable, being grounded in the Ancient Landmarks themselves. It is because they are thus sovereign in their own sphere that a Grand Lodge itself is possible—a Lodge of Lodges, because otherwise there would be nothing in any community except a branch of a Grand Lodge, and therefore the Grand Lodge would be the only Lodge in a State. There is no question here of any rivalry in authority nor of possible conflict, nor can such a conflict or rivalry arise; the two Bodies, the Lodge and the Grand Lodge, belong to the body of Freemasonry as a whole and they are therefore what it has made them, and since this is so Freemasonry cannot be at war with itself. In the majority of other organizations where a "local" body is "subordinate" to an "upper" body an officer in the subordinate may feel himself "lower" than an officer in the "upper" one; this can not be so in Freemasonry; a Worshipful Master is not "lower" than a Grand Master, but is merely at work in Masonry in another way and at another place.

A Lodge has a jurisdiction of its own which no other Lodge can share with it. In cities where two or more Lodges meet and work near each other they have Concurrent Jurisdiction. The territorial limits in such a case are the same for each; but each of them has complete jurisdiction over its own members and petitioners and in respect of them is as independent of its near neighbor Lodges as if they were in another territory. Lodges having concurrent jurisdiction comprise but a small per cent of the total number of Lodges in America; the great majority have complete local jurisdiction. This jurisdiction has boundaries recognized and authorized by the Grand Lodge; a petitioner must have had residence for a certain period within those boundaries; and the Lodge has complete authority over its own members in its Jurisdiction, a measure of authority over members of other Lodges removed to its own jurisdiction, and a larger measure of authority over its own members who have removed outside its own jurisdiction. In one sense it makes little difference to a Mason if he is not a member of the Lodge in the neighborhood where he resides; in another sense it makes much, because each Mason owes a duty to the Fraternity, one pledged by him at the time of his obligation, to attend Lodge, have a voice and a vote in it, and to accept his share in Masonic work—were he to argue that he does his share by paying dues the answer is that the Lodge members who do Lodge work also pay dues.

If Freemasonry were engineered and promoted as some societies and organizations are, it would send a promoter into a community to drum up members and he would be followed by officials from "headquarters" to set up the local body and to start it on its way. They would be very efficient, those officials, and the burden of their speeches would be, "We want you local people to make a success of it," naturally enough—since they receive commissions on every member. There has never been anything of that sort in Freemasonry since its beginning, nor any propagation of any other sort, or promotion. If there are seven Master Masons resident in a community, who are in good standing in regular Lodges, and if they have the endorsement of the adjacent Lodges, they can petition the Grand Lodge for a Dispensation to form a new Lodge, and will do so voluntarily, and without any pressure or persuasion from Grand Lodges or other Lodges. They must show that there is a need for a new Lodge; must designate the place in which it will meet, and must name the three principal officers. This Lodge can then meet, make Masons, and carry on Masonic work, as a "lodge under Dispensation," and will do so for some stated period, at the end of which, it having been inspected and approved, the Grand Lodge may issue to it a charter, or Warrant of Constitution. This Charter becomes effective after the Lodge is consecrated and its room or building is dedicated, and after it has been constituted by the Grand Master or his proxy—thereby obtaining legal status, and its officers have been invested and installed. From then on it has a name and number of its own on the Grand Lodge rolls. In these proceedings from beginning to end the fact stands out clear and plain that the initiative is taken throughout by the seven or more Master Masons who prayed for a Dispensation, and they took that initiative out of their interest in and love for Freemasonry; it is because of this fact that Freemasonry is said to be self-perpetuating, self-propagating, and that Lodges and Grand Lodges are created by Freemasonry, and Freemasonry not by them.

A duly constituted Lodge carries on the work of ancient Craft Masonry and transacts whatever business may be incidental to it. It has a representation in Grand Lodge. In token of such authority as is inherent in it and therefore is underived and inalienable, it remains in possession of its own Charter (or Warrant), which it keeps on its walls, and which can be taken from it only after it has been legally proved unwilling or unfit to carry on the work of a Lodge, and then only by Grand Lodge and under due process of Masonic law. The Lodge admits its own new members by initiation or demission; elects and installs its own officers; can discipline its own members; can levy taxes on them in the form of dues, or fees; makes its own by-laws; and has penal jurisdiction over its own members and over unaffiliated Masons in its jurisdiction.

Such is a Lodge as it is described in the technical language of jurisprudence. If a Mason were to describe a

Lodge as he knows it out of his own knowledge of it from within; he would begin his description elsewhere, and with the feeling that a Lodge is less like a machine and more like a home. It is, in a sense, what Masonry is to him day by day; a place to go; men to be with; acquaintances and friends to have; a large number of interests; and a warmth of free fellowship which he has not elsewhere. It is in those senses his Masonic home, and he calls it that without false sentimentalism. There are some things in Masonry that are not of the sort which come under laws, offices, regulations, or business, but are of the mind and the spirit, and these are of the essence of a Lodge. So with a Grand Lodge; for it is itself more than its machinery of organization, and comes to be more than that for Masons in its Grand Jurisdiction who have any place in it: they, like a Lodge member, find that, from within, a Grand Lodge is not a system of offices and of business but rather is a center for the Masonic spirit as that spirit belongs to the Fraternity as a whole, and without regard to Jurisdictional boundaries. By "Masonic spirit" it is not meant that something in Masonry is too elusive to be captured, but that it is too large to be confined to any particular organization.

Between a Grand Lodge and a Lodge where there might otherwise be a wide gap—there is in every Grand Jurisdiction a network of offices and officers and of special sorts of work which, like a web, knits the Grand Lodge to its Lodges day by day, and, to use another metaphor, is a system of service which run backward and forward between the two. There is in this network, in its details, a general conformity to circumstances which obtain in the Grand Jurisdiction; for that reason it differs from one Grand Jurisdiction to another, but regardless of details it is in every instance the same in substance. Viewed from one end, each line in that network is a means by which the Lodges work with and for the Grand Lodge; viewed from the other end; it is the means by which the Grand Lodge works with and for the Lodges. Thus far Masonic jurisprudence has not given this net-work a name but for our own convenience here, and without the purpose of adding it to Masonic nomenclature, we may describe it as *internal comity*—"comity," in the sense of being a general and continuous co-operation; "internal," in the sense of lying within the Grand Jurisdiction.

In no Grand Jurisdiction has internal comity been developed to a point of completeness; indeed, there are some in which it can scarcely be said to have been begun; it differs much from one to another and therefore it is not possible for any one description to cover forty-nine Grand Jurisdictions. In one of the larger Grand Jurisdictions, however, it has been developed to a point where there is in it almost every element or method that is found in any other. We describe it here for the sake of convenience and not one to be taken as a model.

This particular Grand Jurisdiction is divided into a series of Districts with an average of some sixteen to twenty Lodges in each one. In the larger cities a District consists of its list of Lodges and has no boundaries of its own; outside the cities, it consists of the Lodges in two counties usually, though sometimes only of one. The list of Lodges and the territorial boundaries are in every instance determined by the Grand Lodge. At the very beginning of his term a newly-elected Grand Master appoints for each of them a District Deputy Grand Master, who is his own personal representative, and who can act and speak for him among the Lodges in that District. Such a District Deputy officially inspects each Lodge at least once during the year; he can make an official visit to a Lodge at any time, however, and when he does, needs not to request admittance but can "announce that he is about to enter." When he is in a Lodge it is as if the Grand Master were there in person. At the end of the year each District Deputy makes a written report to the Grand Master; he has a seat and a vote in the Grand Communication: has the title of "Right Worshipful": after his term of office is over, he is likely to remain in Grand Lodge work, for the majority of Grand Officers and Grand Lodge Committee members are chosen from among Past District Deputy Grand Masters. By means of this system a Grand Master can be personally responsible for the supervision of hundreds of Lodges over a large territory where without it it would be impossible for him to visit all the Lodges.

In this Grand Lodge is a Standing Committee, called "Board of Custodians," which has (in the name of the Grand Lodge) responsibility for supervising and inspecting the ritualistic work in the Lodges. This Board employs, as its field respresevative and for full time, an agent who is at the same time a Grand Officer and is appointed by the Grand Master at an annual salary in addition to his expenses. This Grand Lecturer in turn appoints an Assistant Grand Lecturer in each District whose duty it is to inspect the ritualistic work in his own group of Lodges and who is assistant to the Grand Lecturer when, once a year, he comes to inspect the District. The Grand Lecturer makes a report at each stated Grand Communication to the effect that the Lodges are without exception practicing the Standard Uniform Work, and are not introducing into it innovations of their own or permitting themselves to fall beneath a high standard of excellence. The District Deputy Grand Master is continually and immediately responsible to the Grand Master; A District Grand Lecturer is immediately responsible to the Grand Lecturer, and he in turn to the

Grand Master, Neither their responsibilities nor their duties overlap.

In each District, with few exceptions, is a "leader" of another kind who is difficult to describe because he holds no office, carries no title, makes no reports, and carries on from year to year unofficially and informally. Generally, he is a Past Grand Officer who has worked so long in his District that he knows each Lodge in detail and has a personal acquaintanceship with every present and past Lodge officer, and at the same time is equally experienced in Grand Lodge affairs: he is a Nestor, an "elder statesman," and is consulted on such matters as are not official and which, though they may be important in Lodge activities, are personal and private. He has tact and wisdom, and assists to keep his Dictrict in peace and harmony. He cannot be described as belonging to the system of internal comity but his leadership carried on year by year is of great use to it. So also is the work, also unofficial in most instances, of the Past Grand Masters. When his term is ended, a Grand Master does not step to one side to rest on his honors even though "Past Grand Master" is a title and not an office; he has occupied the offices in some Lodge, has served as a District Deputy Grand Master, has occupied each of at least four offices in Grand Lodge, and for one or two years has been Grand Master; that knowledge and skill is of too much worth to be left unused, therefore a Past Grand Master usually will be a Grand Committee Chairman, or have some other Grand Lodge official task: but far more important, he will be a general leader in the area of the State in which he resides, where he will be a colleague of the Grand Master in state-wide Masonic work and will sit in council with him. Meanwhile there are a number of Grand Lodge Committees which carry on services among the Lodges—social, educational, charitable, etc., and they have in hand much that could not come under the care of regular officers. Therefore, by means of the system of internal comity in both its official and unofficial aspects, this Grand Jurisdiction becomes a single, organic whole, working and living as a unit, with members, Lodges, Districts, and the Grand Lodge in one harmonious unit that "neither slumbers nor sleeps" and is never at conflict with itself, a single, vast, collective endeavor to have Freemasonry in its State powerful, prosperous, and happy.

Among the Lodge, District, and Grand Lodge offices required for such a system of internal comity, the first in every sense of the word is the office of Grand Master. Almost every society or organization in America has an officer which it calls by some such name as "president," or "chairman," "head," or "chief," or "executive." An American is familiar with what that office usually consists of, what its functions are, what is expected of its incumbent, and it is natural for him to have that knowledge in mind when he turns to study the office of Grand Master, and he will assume that the chief office in Freemasonry will, in essentials, be similar to the chief office in other societies and organizations. Many things thus far published about the office of Grand Master have gone on that assumption. But the assumption is a mistaken one. A Grand Master is not a president; not a chairman; not merely an executive; his office is unique, unlike any other, not only in detail but in fundamental principles, and for that reason cannot be described in terms generally applicable to other societies but must be described in terms of itself. There is a sense in which it can not even be described as an "office" for though that name is in common use, and though a Grand Master has duties that are "official" in the accepted sense, nevertheless his position in the Craft is less an office than an institution. Certain of his responsibilities are assigned to him by the Grand Lodge, certain of his powers are of a delegated kind, but for the most part his powers, and they are great, are inherent in his position, and have been so from the beginning.

On St. John the Baptist's Day in 1717 four old Lodges in the City of London met at the "Goose and Gridiron" tavern (only inns and taverns in that period provided rooms for such purposes) resolved to erect what later was called a Grand Lodge. To inaugurate it they chose from among themselves the oldest Master Mason present ("now the Master of a Lodge") and placed him "in the chair." He in turn proposed a list of candidates for the Grand Lodge, "and the Brethren by a majority of hands elected Mr. Anthony Sayer, Gentleman, Grand Master of Masons, who being forthwith invested with the Badges of office and power by the said oldest Master, and installed, was duly congratulated by the assembly who paid him the Homage. Mr. Jacob Lamball, a carpenter, and Captain Joseph Elliot were elected Wardens." These facts we have on record in the second edition of the "Book of Constitutions," edited by Dr. James Anderson, published in 1738.

This was the first Grand Lodge and therefore was the origin of the Fraternity of Speculative Freemasonry as it now exists; and since every succeeding Grand Lodge has been in succession from it what was there done has in substance been the law of the Craft ever since. If anything is certain therefore it is that first a Grand Master was selected, and that afterwards a Grand Lodge was constituted. Here in America at the present time that procedure would be reversed; in our Masonic societies a convention of delegates would be held with a set of temporary presiding officers; a written constitution would be adopted, and it would provide for permanent offices and would describe their powers; afterwards these officers would be elected and installed. The ancient traditions of Free-masonry are wholly otherwise. The powers and authorities of the Grand Master, most of them, are "inherent," there-fore belong to the Ancient Landmarks; therefore his of-fice goes back not to Grand Lodge action but to the ancient customs of the Craft, hence he is not a "creature" of Grand Lodge and, in the sphere reserved to him, is not subservient to it. If this be true, if his office be, like a Lodge or a Grand Lodge, an "institution" with original powers of its own, in what way does his spere differ from that of a Grand Lodge? The difference is suggested by the name of the office, which is "Grand Master of Masons," not, "Grand Master of the Grand Lodge"; when among the Lodges, or in the Grand Jurisdiction outside the Lodges, something arises which involves Masons, and solely in their capacity as Masons, and at the same time has a significance more than tempo-rary and more than local, it comes under the Grand Mas-ter's jurisdiction; and it does not come under the Grand Lodge's because it is not of the sort that may be discussed and decided in a Grand Communication.

The Grand Master has the power to convene the Grand Lodge. Excepting for stated Grand Communications, dates for which are provided in the Constitution, no regular and official session of a Grand Lodge can be called except by the Grand Master, in due form, at a time and place specified by him, and for some special purpose or in an emergency, as when a corner-stone is to be laid, or a Grand Lodge funeral service. The Grand Master (or one deputized by him) presides at every session of a Grand Communication, and he may at will preside over any assembly of the Craft or over any Committee, or even over any informal gath-ering; and if he visits a Lodge he enters without invitation and is escorted immediately to the East where, unless he return the gavel to the Worshipful Master, he presides over the Lodge; and this procedure goes on the principle that he can never be subordinate to any other officer at any time or place. The Grand Master is, in respect of the prerogatives of his office, "Grand Master of Masons" in every sense; for not only can he convene the Grand Lodge, the Lodge, a Committee, or any selected group, preside over them, or visit them at will, he can also command or instruct any individual Mason, or any group of Masons anywhere or under any auspices, if they are acting in the name of Masonry, or if what they are doing may reflect upon the name of the Fraternity, or may affect the Craft at large, or is in violation of Masonic purposes and Landmarks; it is thus, as already said, that through him, the Grand Lodge reaches out to each and every Mason inside the Grand Jurisdiction.

Committees in Grand Lodge are appointed by the Grand Master (with one or two possible exceptions) and in doing that,—he reserves to himself the right to preside at will over any one of them, and is an *ex officio* member of each. He also appoints the officers of Grand Lodge who are not elected at the Stated Grand Communication, and, once they are in place, he can summon them, can require information from them, can inspect their papers and reports, and is in such control of them that if one of them is acting improperly he can remove him. In granting a Dispensation for the formation of a new Lodge he follows a procedure in the written law, yet, since the document is powerless without his signature,—he must himself deem it wise and expedient. And so with suspending a Lodge charter; he can act only as the law directs, but it is for him to decide whether to act or not. At the beginning of a Stated Grand Communication the Grand Master reads a message to the Craft in which he reports what he has done during the past year as acting under such rights, prerogatives, and powers as the above, and he can also recommend to the Grand Lodge that it discuss and act upon certain measures he believes to be required, and he also makes it clear what he has found the "state of the Craft" to be; in some respects the decisions he has made, or the opinions he has written, do not come under Grand Lodge review, but where any one of them has had a bearing on Grand Lodge law or practice it will be reviewed by the Grand Lodge, and may be adopted as a permanent statement for the future. A Grand Master's opinions, decisions, and edicts thus belong to the general body of Masonic Jurisprudence and possess, after his term of office, degrees of weight or authority according to the nature of each one. In one respect he is nothing more than an officer of Grand Lodge; in another respect, as was said in an earlier page, his office is independent. If so, it is because a Grand Lodge cannot convene for purposes of legislation and judicial decision oftener than (generally) once a year; he is in a sense the Grand Lodge as it remains in action continuously throughout the year, in every Lodge, and wherever a Mason may be.

A man from the outside who views the office of Grand Master in an impersonal feeling and having in mind the long list of his honors, powers, prerogatives, and privileges would possibly assume that it would have a great appeal for men of ambition, and that such a man might make use of it for purposes of his own. But it is otherwise, seen from within. A Grand Master must be a many-sided man, a public speaker, a leader, a hard worker; be judicious, and yet have in himself a deep and abiding feeling for Freemasonry. Since he came to his position after years of service in other offices, through the Lodge, the District, and the Grand Lodge, including work in Committees, he has a knowledge of the Craft of an exhaustive kind; and even this official experience is not all, because during his services in Grand Lodge offices and Committees he has been associated with other men of a large knowledge of the Craft, and in every branch of its activities. Meanwhile it is required of him, during his term as Grand Master, that he shall travel much, devote a large part of his time to his duties, and, though he has a certain sum available for expenses, it is usual for him to spend much more than that sum out of his own pocket. He is for such reasons a man beyond the majority in respect of his abilities and of his knowledge of Freemasonry; and since each Grand Lodge has many tasks for its Past Grand Masters, he continues in its service throughout the remaining years of his life. A Grand Master himself, in what he is in his mind and character, is as important to the Grand Lodge as the duties and functions of his office; he is never merely an incumbent, dutifully performing a number of set duties, but is also Grand Master in his own proper person as well as in the sense that he holds an office by that name.

When we turn from the office of Grand Master to the office of Worshipful Master a certain superficial similarity comes at once into view, as if a Worshipful Master were a Grand Master *in petto,* as if there were no difference in principle between the two, and that what a Grand Master is in a large sphere, a Worshipful Master is in a small one. But there is in this only an appearance of likeness, not the reality, because the two *are different in* kind; and any endeavor to reason from one to the other is necessarily fallacious. There is, in example, a kind of authority which belongs to the office of Grand Master which does not belong to that of Worshipful Master, and it may be roughly described as being an authority to decide what is Masonic and what is not—at some points, and under certain circumstances, he decides concerning the Fraternity itself, rather than on questions that may arise within the Fraternity. Thus, a Grand Master can decide whether a Lodge shall be instituted in a given community or not, and this means, whether that community shall have Masonry in it or not; and to the same effect is his power to suspend a Charter, which is to decide that a given community shall cease to have Masonry in it. A Worshipful Master can make no decisions of that kind; he comes into a Lodge already existing, already formed, already equipped with laws, regulations, and offices, and he must accept it as he finds it, and his place in it is one already provided for, and defined, and he cannot alter it. He has power, it is great power, in its own sphere it is original and inalienable, belonging to the Ancient Landmarks; a Grand Lodge, nor a Grand Master, can not take it away from him, and it is not a power delegated to him by his Lodge, nevertheless, it is a power solely confined to seeing that the work of a Lodge is carried on as the Landmarks, Constitutions, and general regulations require that it shall be and does not permit him to decide about Freemasonry in general or matters affecting the Grand Jurisdiction as a whole.

The Constituent Lodge procedure is adjusted traditionally to a year which begins on one St. John the Evangelist's Day (December 27th) and ends on the next. Lodge and Grand Lodge dues are paid for that period; the Lodge's reports to Grand Lodge usually cover that period; the terms of Lodge office conform to it, and the installation of new officers is held as near to it as possible, because the old officers continue until their successors are installed. A Mason can refuse to accept an office but once he has accepted and has been installed, he cannot resign, because what he accepted was, condensed into a term, a year-in-office, and it was for that set term that he was installed: if he removes from the community or is hampered by illness,—a substitute is appointed until the next election. An officer's incumbency ends only when his term expires, or he dies, or is expelled (which is Masonic death). In some Grand Jurisdictions there are local and special rules governing these matters relating to offices for which reason it is impossible to give a detailed description of them which will hold for each and every Grand Jurisdiction; but the principles in each one, its place and function in the Craft, are the same in every Grand Jurisdiction.

The office of Worshipful Master is among the oldest in Masonry, and it is probable that the first Lodge ever organized had such an officer, though he may have been called by another name. "Worshipful" is from the same Anglo-Saxon root as "worthy" and has been used as a term of respect in Europe and Britain for more than a thousand years—even at the present time an English countryman is likely to employ "worshipful" as we employ "sir"; it is therefore unconnected with the word "worship" as used in the churches. "Master" has the meaning of being in control of a body of men, and is also in Masonry further defined as one who has mastered Masonry as an art. As a title it carries the double implication of being an officer who is the executive head of the Lodge entitled to respect and obedience and therefore the Master of the Lodge, and at the same time has authority in certain respects over the members individually and therefore is Master of Masons. In each of these aspects of his office he has powers and prerogatives which belong to him inherently, are among the Ancient Landmarks, are not conferred on him by written laws or by action of Lodges or Grand Lodges, are neither given nor taken away; for such reasons his office is, in a sense employed in the nomenclature of our jurisprudence, an Institution, and is so as truly as is a Lodge, a Grand Lodge, or the office of Grand Master.

In the previous chapter you were reminded what is required of a Worshipful Master in the way of interior preparation, of knowledge, thought, feeling, of personal graces and of moral qualifications. The office is one of great laboriousness. A man must devote from three to seven years to the subordinate offices before he reaches it; in it he must preside over the Lodge each time it is in Communication, must supervise its business, its records, its finance, must arrange for special Communications; he must be a Ritualist who will spend many nights in Lodge assisting to confer Degrees, in which his is the largest portion of work and many nights at home reviewing, or relearning, ceremonies, Special Services, or portions of the Degrees; he is in continuous service on Committees, both standing and special, is called upon, by his members for innumerable purposes and at unexpected times; and meanwhile must act for his Lodge, lead it, and speak for it, or represent it in Grand Lodge and among neighboring Lodges and in the community.

In truth, a Worshipful Master of an American Lodge of two hundred or more members has too much to do, and it would be a mercy to him and an act of wise statesmanship for the Craft if Lodges and Grand Lodges were to recover, and to put again into practice, more of the duties which originally belonged to the two Wardens, that a Lodge may not make so excessive a demand on the time and strength of its principal officer. There is in the whole of Freemasonry nothing more extraordinary than the fact that each year some sixteen thousand American Lodges are able to find that many men willing and prepared to accept this office which takes out of them so much and yet gives them in return neither salaries, nor even, except in part, their expenses; it is a testimony to the existence in Freemasonry of some secret appeal or inward fascination which it has for men who work for it from within, and which appears to increase of itself the more they increase their labors for it.

The duties of a Worshipful Master correspond, point to point, to the facets and phases of Lodge work. He personally is custodian of the Lodge charter, and must make sure to hand it on to his successor in good condition. He is executive head of his Lodge and must preside over it when it is assembled, and must call it into special Communication when in his judgment that is called for. He appoints the appointive officers, and also the chairmen and members of Standing and Special Committees, with a few exceptions. If he is not able to be present at a Lodge Communication he must provide for another to act for him, but it is expected of him that he shall be in attendance except for extraordinary reasons. He opens the Lodge, and closes it, and is responsible to do both at an appointed time, a duty which may require of him that he be at the Lodge room an hour before his members, or remain an hour or two after they have left—he is wise to discharge this duty meticulously, for few things are more trying to an assembly of men than to be tardy in beginning and unnecessarily late in closing. When presiding over his Lodge the Master decides questions of order, and decides whether a proposal made from the floor is in the Order of Business or not. If a vote is a tie he casts the deciding vote. When vacancies in office occur during the year, it is for him to make *pro tem* appointments to fill them. It is for him to decide whether visitors are admitted or not, and, if admitted, to welcome them, taking care to do so according to the established ceremonies when visitors are Lodge or Grand Lodge officers, which may mean to surrender his gavel if the visitor is a Grand Master or a District Deputy Grand Master.

He is expected at each opportunity, as the charges to a

Master have it, not only to "set the Craft to work" but also to "instruct them" in their labors, which may in practice be, to expound points of Masonic law, to review Grand Lodge Proceedings or to explain phrases or portions of the Ritual or the customs and privileges of members. It is his duty to sign the Lodge Minutes, to sign orders on the Treasurer, and to draw orders for Grand Lodge dues and for Masonic relief. It is among the first of his responsibilities, which the Opening Ceremonies do not ever permit him to forget, to make sure that "peace and harmony prevail" among his members (the majority of the few instances of the removal of Worshipful Masters from their office has been because of their failure at this vital point); therefore he must "head off" schisms and quarrels before they arise, enforce the laws impartially and promptly, and if a member be brought to answer for un-Masonic conduct, to make sure for him of a fair trial. If members are in arrears with their dues, or with other fees or moneys owed the Lodge, it is for him to collect them. He is custodian of the Lodge property, in most instances as assisted by the Trustees, and must see that it is kept in repair, and is clean and comfortable, and is protected by insurance. At a time specified by his Grand Lodge Code, he must see that Grand Lodge returns are made to the Grand Secretary. When a Masonic burial is requested by the family of a deceased Mason he is in charge of the ceremonies and arrangements. He sits in Grand Communications as the representative of the Lodge, perhaps with one or two of his Wardens with him—if the Grand Lodge laws so provide (which some do, and some do not). He serves Lodge notices, issues summonses. In assemblies of his Lodge, his is the last word in the control of debates, and whatever he decides from the East is final; no appeal can be made from him to the floor, and in most Grand Jurisdictions any appeal from his acts or decisions of any kind must be made to the Grand Master or to Grand Lodge. At the end of his term he installs his successor, perhaps with a ceremony which it has taken him an evening to learn.

In the meantime, and over and above these official duties, he will be expected to address his own Lodge, or possibly a neighboring Lodge, at regular Communications, at banquets, or at other unofficial assemblies, and to do so in the consciousness that he is a public speaker not in his own name only but also as the spokesman or the representative of his Lodge, which duty, and though it is not official, may, if he is not a practiced speaker be his most trying ordeal—since to fail is to embarass his Brethren. And while at this duty, as at all others, he is expected to be a master of etiquette, a model of decorum, groomed to befit his station, and practiced in the social arts. If these duties be not sufficient he can find in another direction, wholly apart and away from institutional affairs, another world in which to work; for the members of his Lodge are also his brothers, acquaintances, and friends, and if one be ill, or is in mourning, or is in trouble otherwise, the Master will feel it to be a call upon himself—and do it gladly—to visit them and to bring to them relief, succor, condolence or good will from their Lodge.

When you come to the end of such a description of the duties and prerogatives of the office of the Worshipful Master as is given in the paragraphs immediately above, and which is found in Codes, handbooks, and works on Masonic jurisprudence in a numbered set of directions or prescriptions, you may have the impression that there remains nothing more to be said; if an incumbent carries out these established and time-honored duties he will have discharged his office with honor to himself and satisfaction to his Craft. And that impression will be true. Nevertheless if you will reflect upon that set of duties until you have grasped for yourself what each one means in the terms of thought, feeling, action, experience, when it is carried out, and if while so doing you also reflect upon it in the terms of what Freemasonry is as a whole, a new fact will emerge which is one of the secrets of Masonic jurisprudence, one that goes down to the roots of it and illuminates the whole of it. The fact is that while, on the one hand, the duties of the Master are officially stated and enumerated, so that he cannot omit or contravene any one of them and cannot change or alter his office to please himself, on the other hand, and almost at every point, the Master at the same time is free to act upon his own initiative, of his own right, using his own knowledge and judgment to decide what both himself and his Lodge shall do. Stated in the fewest possible words Freemasonry is so organized that at one stroke it provides a maximum of rules, regulation, order, rigidity, and a maximum of freedom, of voluntary endeavor, of private initiative; and it is because this is true of it that it has continued over so many centuries and remained ever the same, and yet has remained alive, progressive, has grown and developed, and has possessed the living loyalty of intelligent men who would not devote themselves to a petrified, rigid system.

A Master can be creative; fertile in new ideas; ingenious in finding new things for his Lodge to do; can exercise his own wits, take the intiative, can keep the work of his Lodge fresh and moving and full of novelty, knowing that Freemasonry is inexhaustible in itself; and when he does so his members will see that these things which he himself does, and so many of which would not be done if he did not take the lead, only carry out to their fulfillment, either in express purpose or in spirit, the fixed rules and regulations by which his office is controlled in law and custom. This

explains the great difference in atmosphere as between
one Lodge and another; the moment a Mason enters a
Lodge he knows whether it is ruled and governed by a
Master who, out of timidity or indifference, leans back on
the mere letter of his duties, content if he can keep the
wheels turning over, or by a Master who has in him the
spirit of leadership and of progress; and at the end of a
Master's year his members will judge of it, whether it has
been prosperous or not according as he has been one or
the other. And it is for this reason that it is so often said
by men who are authorities in the philosophy of Masonry
that a Master is more than an incumbent of an office, and
that when a Mason is selected by his Brethren to hold the
title, he is selected as much for what he is privately as a
man, in character, soul, and ability as for his fitness to
carry out duties and prescriptions. An excellent book to
assist the Master in the conduct of his office and to get the
best results is "Masonic Lodge Methods" by L. B. Blake-
more.

The Senior Warden is the ranking officer next after the
Worshipful Master. He is also, in general Lodge practice
though not in law, the heir presumptive; the prospective
Master, and this fact though impalpable and assumed
rather than stated, has weight in giving shape to the character and feeling of his office. 1. The office of Senior
Warden is a fixed, inalterable part of the structure of a
Lodge organization, and for that reason is partly constitutive of what a Lodge is—a Lodge without a Senior
Warden would be no Lodge at all; the office is not a detachable one, nor one alterable either by its incumbent or
by the Lodge, and its duties belong, directly or indirectly,
among the Ancient Landmarks. The question "What will
the office of Senior Warden be if so-and-so is elected to it?"
can never arise: the question invariably is, "Would so-

and-so be qualified to hold the office of Senior Warden?"
2. The incumbent holds the office of Senior Warden; the office itself has a station in the Lodge room, a fixed place always in the West, and in it center many activities of the Lodge when assembled in Regular Communication or while conferring a Degree. Many of the particular forms of work of a Lodge may be carried on here and there, in this place or in that, now or then, outside the Lodge room or in it, and often as the Brother doing it may decide for himself and perhaps at his own convenience; but a Senior Warden, in order to carry on his own work, must not only be present in Lodge and at a stated time but must remain in his own station throughout, and if he be a restless or an impatient man, he is miscast for the office.

3. The Senior Warden is the second ranking officer. In a large sense he is the vice–, or deputy-Master; would, in theory, take the Master's place when the Master is absent from his own station, but, in practice, Masonic law, in both the theory of it and in the written forms of it, has never yet crystallized at this point; the laws and practices vary from one Grand Jurisdiction to another—the practices sometimes vary from one Lodge to another. If it be alleged that the Senior Warden should of right occupy the East whenever the Master is absent from his station, then it would necessarily follow that the officer in each station and place would also have to advance to the office next above, because no station or place can be left unoccupied, and this would occasion too much confusion. 4. The Senior Warden has one of the largest and most important parts in the Opening and Closing ceremonies and in the Ritual of the Degrees. 5. In a number of Grand Jurisdictions he is by virtue of his office a standing committee on Masonic relief, or on charity (in Masonry the two are not the same) ; in a number of others, where the Principal Officers

constitute a Board of Relief, he is its chairman. 6. Along with the Master he is usually entitled to represent his Lodge in Grand Lodge and to have a voice and a vote in Grand Communications; in Grand Jurisdictions where he does not have a seat in Grand Lodge it is not because his right to have one is denied but because the number of Lodges is so large that a plural representation from each and every Lodge could not be seated in the Grand Lodge Room. 7. Also, by virtue of a duty inherent in his office, he is responsible for seeing that decorum is maintained; in discharging this duty, which might call him away from his station he can act through the Junior Deacon, who is his proxy, as the Senior Deacon is similarly the Worshipful Master's proxy.

The office of Senior Warden is as old as the office of Worshipful Master. Written Operative Masonic records of as early as the Thirteenth Century show that even then a Lodge had Wardens, and it is likely that the office, though perhaps not called by its present name, belonged to the first Lodges ever organized. From that time on, it has ever been an established doctrine in Masonic Jurisprudence that next after his duty to act as the Master's second in rank, the principal duty of the Senior Warden has been to "set the Craft to work" and a statement to this effect is embedded in the Opening Ceremony and is everywhere taken for granted in the Ritual of the Three Degrees. But in the custom of the great majority of American Lodges the practice of this duty has fallen into disuse, or is overlooked, or neglected, or forgotten, or at best is put into a half-hearted practice. It was stated on an earlier page that in the usual way of things the Worshipful Master has too many duties, too many demands on himself, and is therefore overworked, which is an injustice of which no Masonic Lodge ought ever to be guilty, or else he must let go by default many forms of work which a normal and prosperous Lodge requires. This has partly come about because so many of the tasks traditionally belonging to the Senior Warden have been transferred to the Master, leaving the office of Senior Warden emasculated and only half efficient.

There is at this point a duty for Masonic statesmanship. In the principles of Masonic organization each and every Lodge member is expected to have a part in the work of the Lodge; and he is furthermore expected to be willing to be assigned, or "told off," to his task by whatever officer may have that responsibility; this is made clear to a Candidate during his initiation and he himself pledges himself to it while taking his obligation—he is to have a post of duty and when summoned to it he is in honor bound to obey the summons. The whole Craft therefore is to be at labor, not leaving Lodge work to a chosen few, and it is for the Senior Warden not only to superintend the Craft while thus at labor but also to see that no man fails of his duty, and furthermore to see that each man has an assigned post of duty for himself and is not left to wander aimlessly about wondering what there is for him to do. If this responsibility of the Senior Warden were recalled and made effectual, it would relieve the Master of burdens which of right he should not be expected to carry; it would result in an active, vigorous, working Lodge in which there would be no idle and discontented members and therefore would be no non-attendance problem. He is also placed there to see that "harmony prevails."

The office of Junior Warden ranks next after that of Senior Warden. Here again, strangely enough, we have a case where an ancient, traditional duty, stated in the Ritual and provided for in the Ancient Landmarks, has among our American Lodges been set aside, and has been so at the cost of Lodge vitality and with the result that certain tasks which ought to be done by the Junior Warden have been transferred to the Worshipful Master. From the beginning the principal duty of the Junior Warden has been to hold a station in which many activities center when the Brethren are assembled in business Communication or to confer a Degree; ranking only next after that is his duty to superintend the Craft when at Refreshment. In an American Lodge "Refreshment" denotes many and various activities, the members, when at Lodge, in the intervals of work, members in the anteroom, the lobby, or their club room, when at meals or lunches, entertainments, banquets, dances, parties, picnics, and programs of speeches or other methods by which the Lodge carries on its educational work. Why then should a Lodge have a Social (or Entertainment) Committee? Why a Special Committee each time a special occasion is desired? The Junior Warden already is a Permanent Social Committee by virtue of his office, and on any strict construction of Masonic law, any other Committee which trespasses on his office is out of order; if such Committees are needed he should appoint them and afterwards should preside over them and be responsible to the Lodge for what they do— if he is not adequate to that amount of responsibility what is he to do when in two more years (other things being equal) he becomes Worshipful Master with responsibility for a whole Lodge! And if to be responsible for the whole social and entertainment side of the Lodge be the second most important duty of his office why not let him discharge that duty? Why should it be transferred to the Worshipful Master, or a Committee?

The Treasurer has a place in the East at the right of the Worshipful Master. His Jewel is a pair of crossed keys, which are to remind him and the Craft that the Lodge's funds are kept securely. It is his duty to receive monies from the Secretary; to see that they are promptly banked: to keep records of them: to dispense sums at the will and pleasure of the Worshipful Master; and consent of the Lodge and to be ready to give a statement about finances when called upon.

In one respect and to a certain extent what was said about the lost prerogatives or duties of the offices of the two Wardens is true of the office of Treasurer. He also has come to have an emasculated office. During the long centuries of Operative Masonry he was responsible for the care and disbursement of Lodge funds, as he still is, but he was also in that office in which reposed responsibility to see that Lodge monies were appropriated only for certain specified purposes, and not spent at random. There is a movement under way to recover this ancient use by way of a Lodge Budget. For it is manifestly impossible to keep Lodge expenditures in balance, guaranteeing that no one department of Lodge activity shall receive more than its share of Lodge funds at the expense of some other department—which in practice would mean, to give one example only, to make sure that the Lodge does not spend ten dollars for entertainment, one dollar for Masonic Relief, and nothing for Masonic education. If members are permitted, when in a business Communication, to move appropriations of money without regard to the whole of the needs for a year, or of the needs of other sorts, the Lodge's use of its funds is thrown out of balance, and it is impossible to maintain a complete program of activities— and, as it often turns out, it is therefore difficult to avoid a deficit at the end of a year. If a Lodge adopts a budget it calculates at the beginning of the year the total amount of money to be available during the year, it allocates certain fixed portions of this to each of the departments, and permits no department to overdraw its own share except by special action of the Lodge, since the budget was officially adopted by the Lodge. Where the Lodge employs the Budget System the chairmanship of it belongs by nature to the Treasurer.

The office of Secretary is by common consent second in importance only after that of Worshipful Master; and even the Master does not come into contact so often with the members individually, or with so many of them, or at so many points, wherefrom arises the old and tried saying, "A Secretary can make or break a Lodge." In reality he is three Secretaries at one stroke, for he is Recording Secretary, Financial Secretary, and Corresponding Secretary. He receives and reads all communications addressed to the Lodge or to himself as its Secretary, and replies to same either according to his own judgment, in some instances, or, as in most cases, according to instructions from the Master or the Lodge. Prepares, issues and mails notices, summonses, statements, etc.; cares for certain routine communications, oftentimes of a stated and official character, between his Lodge and Grand Lodge.

He keeps the accounts as between the Lodge and each of its members, issues statements for dues, receives dues, keeps records of dues owing or paid, files lists of delinquents, receives and records initiation and special fees or assessments, transmits all monies received to the Treasurer and keeps a record of them in his own books. At each Stated or Special Communication of his Lodge he keeps minutes, reads them at the end, and if they are approved signs them, has the Master sign them, and preserves them in the archives. During Communications he often is called upon for information, or to read a letter, or is consulted about past Lodge actions, therefore having an active part in Lodge business. He keeps a register of the members, a visitors' book, prepares dimits, diplomas, etc., when authorized, attends trials for recording evidence, is custodian of the seal of the Lodge, notifies the Grand Secretary of suspensions and expulsions, is responsible for the keeping in safety and good order all papers, books, etc., belonging to the Lodge and for delivering them to his successor. In some Grand Jurisdictions he must give bond; in every Grand Jurisdiction he usually is continued year to year in office (*mutatis mutandis*), often dying in harness; if he receives pay for his work it is not given as a salary but as a stipend, a method employed to protect him against financial loss to himself, and with no thought ever that it is adequate compensation for his giving more time and more work to his Lodge than any other officer in it.

The Deacons, as their name and their ensigns of office attest, are messengers, in whose two offices is embodied the idea of work being done outside the Lodge room, either literally or symbolically. The Senior Deacon is both the messenger and the proxy of the Worshipful Master. In the conferring of Degrees he has more floor work than any other officer except the Master, since he acts as conductor for the Candidate, and in doing so acts often as a spokesman for the Candidate. When visitors are admitted by the Tiler it is for him to receive them, to introduce them, and to see that they find seats. He has charge of the ballot box at the time of a balloting. He is in charge of the Masters of Ceremony if his Lodge has such officers and is responsible for seeing that Candidates are properly prepared, and that decorum is not violated either within or without the Inner Door. He speaks and acts in the Master's name, carries about with him the atmosphere of the authority which belongs to the East; it is for him therefore to walk with dignity, handle his rod with precision, speak with firmness and a clear utterance, move along straight lines and turn at right angles. The Junior Deacon is to the Senior Warden what the Senior Deacon is to the Master, an assistant, a messenger, and a proxy, whose place is at the Senior Warden's right, and near the Outer Door, where his duties within it complement the Tiler's duties without it, and to see that the Lodge is duly Tiled, to attend to alarms and to report the same.

The Chaplain is not present in the Lodge as pastor, minister, or preacher, but is as his name implies, the incumbent of an office; and since so, the office itself should be clearly defined in his mind, its duties, and the decorum attached to it; as an office its functions have their point in those portions of the Ceremonies and the Ritual which center in the Altar, the Bible, and Prayers. It is therefore out of keeping with the nature of a Lodge for it to have no such office, no trained officer to fill it, and to depend on hit or miss. There is in the whole of the work a basis in reverence; and there is in its enactment a need for an officer to so conduct and regulate the Lodge as to secure that there shall be no irreverence. He sits on the Master's right.

STEWARDS

In the early days of Speculative Lodges in England, when a Lodge room was as often as not a banquet room, and when a "feast" was the climax of a "meeting" the two stewards were charged with the responsibility of securing the food, having it prepared and served, and of keeping account of table expenses. Next in order of importance, it was their duty to prepare the Lodge room for each Communication. Also, at various times and in divers countries, they have collected dues and fees, introduced visitors, and assisted the higher officers in their work as those officers might require. We have transferred those duties to Committees, to the Tiler, to the Secretary, and, in some instances, to the Deacons, and the result is that their one duty left of large importance is to prepare the Candidate. If so, a modern Lodge Steward need not feel that his is an office of small weight in the Lodge, because there is a period in the experience of a Candidate when he receives an impression of Freemasonry which will remain indelibly fixed in his feelings, and that period is the half hour which he spends in the Preparation Room; for if he there and then receives the impression that Freemasonry is not to be taken seriously, or even that there is buffoonery in it, a man will find it hard to rid himself of that feeling which is an indignity to him and an injustice to the Lodge.

There may come a time when the Stewards may be put in recovery of one of their lost prerogatives, because over the years and over the country the custom of assigning our own "feasts" to Special Committees is not working out with satisfaction; it would be better if the feasts were in the care of these two stated officers of the Lodge who could, because of their authority and out of knowledge accumu-lated in their office, protect a Lodge against those ama-teurish "lunches," improvised at the last moment, which strike a man as a sad reflection on the Lodge's hospitality.

The Tiler (also spelled Tyler) is the Lodge's sentinel and doorkeeper. The name borne by his office is an etymologic mystery; nobody knows when or where it orig-inated or why it was adopted for the guard or warden at the Outer Gate of the Lodge precincts; not even the Royal Philological Society of England, which has sifted every known scrap of data for the history of English words. In some countries and places of the Middle Ages, roofing a building was called tiling, and a roofer was called a tiler; but this does not explain why the doorkeeper of the Lodge was called Tiler. It has been suggested that the word has a symbolic meaning, suggesting that, as a Tiler closed in a building from the outside world, the Tiler is to cut off any inspection of the Lodge room by profanes.

The Tiler's is an office necessary to the existence of a Lodge, without which no Lodge could lawfully assemble and whose absence from his post, even for a moment, would constitute an irregularity in Lodge procedure, yet he has no place in the Lodge room, and is the only Masonic officer stationed in the profane world. He is present before the first member arrives, remains until after the last member has departed, and during the whole of the time has contact at least once with every officer, member, and visitor, yet he is never present in the Lodge room and has no part in what goes on there. He is the first to greet every member who approaches, the first to greet every visitor, is therefore the first to extend the Lodge's hospitality. His emblem of office is the sword. When members approach after the Lodge is opened he makes sure that they are properly clothed and then knocks on the door in signal to the Junior Deacon; if those who approach are not members of the Lodge it is his duty to see that they are vouched for or are examined, that they sign the visitors' book, and are clothed, after which he introduces them to the Junior Deacon. He is but one of a large staff of Lodge officers, in the list of those officers which show their order of precedence he usually stands last, and he has neither place nor function inside the Lodge room itself, and yet as the word is most often used his is the most "official" of any of the offices, and this is as it should be because in the nature of things a Lodge's only point of contact with strangers or visitors from the outside world must be an official one. It is for him to enforce the rules rigorously and in their most literal sense, without fear or favor, making no exceptions, showing no partiality to those with whom he is acquainted or prejudice against those with whom he is not, never deciding for himself as to what a rule should be or when it should be enforced, knowing that to admit a man to the door of the Lodge is never for him privately to decide but for the Master to determine. Therefore it is his sole duty to enforce the rules; and, since he is given the power and the authority to do it, it is never suitable for him to act "officiously"—for to "act officiously" is the exact opposite of acting officially!

The offices of Marshal, Masters of Ceremony, and Pursuivant are not in use in a number of Grand Jurisdictions, in others are optional with the Lodges, and are mandatory in only a small number of Grand Jurisdictions. There is a need here, as you have already found in this discussion under other heads, for Grand Lodges to complete the system of Masonic Jurisprudence, because on the question of the number of required offices both the Written and Unwritten Laws are either silent or else lie in confused ambiguity. There is such a thing as Freemasonry; it can be accurately defined both in details of practice and in those fundamentals of it called the Landmarks; and it either calls for or does not call for a fixed number of offices. If the forty-nine Grand Lodges, through their system of comity were to agree on that fixed number, would they include the offices of Marshal, Masters of Ceremony, and of Pursuivant? It is likely that a large majority would require each and every Lodge to have a Marshal; perhaps less than a majority would require Masters of Ceremony, though many of them would; if the office of Steward were restored to its original purpose, which would not include the preparation of Candidates because it is inconceivable that the preparation of candidates can belong to the same category of duties as the preparation of meals and the custodianship of Lodge gear and properties. Pursuivant would in that case be uncalled for because his duty of caring for regalia and other properties would belong to the Stewards. It could be safely predicted therefore that Marshal would become a required office even with present practices unchanged; and that Masters of Ceremony would sometimes be required but Pursuivant would not be necessary providing that the offices of the stewards were reconstituted.

A Pursuivant is, in principle, nothing more than a Steward, though his custodianship of Lodge properties is usually narrowed down to the care of regalia and such other gear and equipment as belong to that category. Masters of Ceremony are to prepare the Candidate both physically and psychologically, protecting him against unmannered intrusion and preserving him in quiet and dignity, standing with him while the Secretary reads his statement, and presenting him at the Inner Door, and when he returns to the Preparation Room, to receive him again. The Candidate must be prepared in a certain way; since he could not prepare himself, others must assist him to do it, and this is, in the strict sense, an office of the Lodge and men should be appointed to discharge it.

The Marshal, appointed by and acting under the immediate directions of the Worshipful Master, is in control of the movement of the Lodge as a body, when that movement must be in a fixed order. When the officers, visitors, and members walk in line to the table to occupy assigned seats; or when they walk on the streets in ordered procession; or when they go as a body to attend church, or to lay a cornerstone, or dedicate a building, or to consecrate a Lodge room, or to conduct a funeral, or when, as at a Grand Communication, they enter a Lodge room ceremonially, they not only walk in an ordered line but also according to a traditional order or precedence. It is the Marshal's function to maintain this decorum.

The last Masonic office which it falls within our present purpose to discuss is one that does not appear in the lists

given in any of the works of jurisprudence; nor has any
Grand Lodge (unless some Book of Constitutions has been
inadvertently overlooked) ever given it the official status
of an office. What is here said about it therefore is on the
writer's own responsibility. Nevertheless that responsibility can be assumed without too much risk because,
while Grand Lodges and writers on jurisprudence have
never given to it the name of office, they have recognized it
to be one in everything but name; therefore why not give
it that recognition? The office in question is that of "Member." By Member is meant any Master Mason who belongs
to a Lodge and is in good standing in it.

Albert G. Mackey's *Jurisprudence of Freemasonry* has
been for more than three-quarters of a century the standard work on the subject, and since each and every Grand
Lodge has guided itself according to it in countless decisions and legislative acts, it may be described without exag-
geration as the weightiest and most influential Masonic
book ever written by an American; in addition to that
weightiness, it has the distinction of being a literary masterpiece with a permanent place among the small number
of Masonic classics. In Chapter III of Book III of that work
Dr. Mackey described the rights of a Master Mason, and
gives a list of nine of them under headings which though
succinct are completely self-descriptive: 1. The Right of
Membership. 2. The Right of Affiliation. 3. The Right of
Visit. 4. The Right of Avouchment. 5. The Right of Relief.
6. The Right of Demission. 7. The Right of Appeal. 8.
The Right of Burial. 9. The Right of Trial.

Mackey's discussion was confined to limits determined
for him by the purpose of his book, as a whole, and as
described by the title of the chapter in particular: it was
to state what the Craft owes to one of its members. It is
not possible for any man to incorporate in one book the

whole of Masonic jurisprudence, and it is, therefore, not a disparagement of his book to say that in addition to Rights two whole sides of membership belong to any statement of what it is to be a Master Mason; and they are, first, the Duties which belong to it; and, second, the Functions which inhere in it.

The Duties of a Master Mason are either voluntarily accepted by him at the time of taking his Obligations or else are explicitly stated, or are implied, in the laws, rules, and regulations; and they are Duties in the sense that a member is bound to discharge them without respect to his private desires or feelings. Among these are such as: To attend Lodge: To pay dues: To pay fees and assessments: To give to Masonic relief: To accept a part in the work of the Lodge: To obey summones: To respond to the sign of distress: To remain in peace and harmony: To have a voice and to vote: To obey the officers.

Freemasonry, and by virtue of what it is as a living and working Craft carries on many activities and among these are many things which can be done only by members, and cannot be done by anybody else, not by officers or committees or in any of the Stations and Places of the Lodge, nor by assemblies or laws or by paid men brought in from outside. In the organization of the Craft, which is rigidly structuralized from top to bottom, each and every sort of activity must have a place, and this place oftentimes is taken in so literal a sense that it is a place located somewhere in a room, a fact testified to by the words "Stations" and "Places." Among these a member has a place of his own; and since certain of the activities of the Craft are centered in that place it is for a member to carry them on. These activities, which only a member can carry on, and which can be carried on only in the place in Masonry which belongs to him when combined with his Rights and Duties, together constitute an Office, and do so with that term employed in its most correct and adequate sense.

Among the majority of fraternities and societies, with the exceptions being most often found among those fraternities which have patterned themselves upon Freemasonry, there is on one side of them, as it were, a set of offices and officers working within a limited area; within that area everything is rigidly organized and goes according to function and rule; outside of it is a large area which is not organized and in which go-as-you-please is the only rule. Freemasonry has nothing in common with a society of that type. In it are no areas of loose, fluid, unorganized, unregulated, activities. It is an Order, a complete organization in the form of a hierarchy of offices, ranks, grades, titles, places, orders of precedence, and duties, comprehending in one unbroken fabric everything from a chance visitors' hour in a Lodge room, to a Grand Communication of Grand Lodge, everybody from the youngest Entered Apprentice in the newest Lodge to the oldest Past Grand Master; this continues without interruption or cessation day and night, and for ever; and every man who comes into it has a place of his own, and regardless of where a Master Mason stands in it, he stands in an Office.

A Member cannot walk into Lodge at what hour he may chance to do so, through this door or through that, as he may choose, or in what manner it may be his whim to do so, but must come at a stated time, and enter and be received in due form. Once in it he cannot sit where he pleases, but has an assigned place in the side-lines. During the session of the Lodge he cannot rise and speak when he feels moved to do so, nor can he go about carrying on conversations at will, nor move about freely from one place to another. If he is led to desire a part in the work of the

Lodge he cannot hunt out a task to please himself, cannot, if the notion strikes him, join with the Master in the East, or pre-empt a share of the Senior Warden's part in the Opening and Closing Ceremonies; if a Committee is in session he is not free to sit with it at will; nor has he a voice in the functions of any of the Stations or Places, Officers, or Committees. Even outside the Lodge room, and regardless of how footloose he may otherwise be, he is not at liberty to act for his Lodge or in the name of Masonry but is under a rule to act as becomes a Mason, and is penalized if his conduct cannot bear the scrutiny of his superiors in the Craft. If he occupies a post in the work of the Lodge it is his right and duty to do so but he has no right to choose that post for himself, but must ask that one be assigned to him, and he will do it as expected, for Masonic work goes according to functions and places. In sum, he holds an Office of which the title is "Brother," and while it is large enough to offer him a full and complete opportunity for the time, energy, ability, and mind he can bring to it, it is nevertheless an Office, which is therefore in a place of its own among the other Offices of Lodges and Grand Lodges.

CHAPTER III

THE BOOK OF CONSTITUTIONS

THE "Time Immemorial" Lodges before 1717, though independent of each other and without any national center or government for the Craft as a whole, worked harmoniously among themselves because they practiced the same Freemasonry. Each of them used some form of the *Old Charges,* they had modes of recognition in common, the rules and regulations in one Lodge were in substance the same as in any other; etc. Masonic written law was for the government of a local Lodge; the Craft as a whole was guided by unwritten law. When the first Grand Lodge was organized (1717) it was a Masonic body of an unprecedented kind. Where a Lodge had individual Masons for members, the Grand Lodge had Lodges; where a Lodge had a local jurisdiction, a Grand Lodge had the nation. There arose, in consequence, a need for a body of Grand Lodge law. This need was satisfied when, in 1723, the Grand Lodge adopted a code prepared for it by a Committee headed by Reverend James Anderson, and called "The Book of Constitutions."

These Constitutions were a body of law to govern the Grand Lodge itself. It defined the structure of a Grand Lodge; fixed the boundaries of its Grand Jurisdiction; named its Grand Officers and described their duties; provided for the supervision of member Lodges and for the founding of new Lodges; set a limit to Grand Lodge's own authority and at the same time made the member Lodges constituents of the Grand Lodge, and therefore answerable to it; and laid down the rules and regulations by which the Fraternity as a whole was to be governed. The Grand Lodge itself therefore was the subject-matter of "The Book of Constitutions," and within its scope nothing was included except what appertained to its own work and jurisdiction; the Ancient Landmarks continued as before; a Local Lodge continued to govern itself as before except at the point where it had contact with the Grand Lodge, and Freemasonry continued to be what it had always been. It is true that a Grand Lodge was an authority above a Lodge, with power to issue Charters or to recall them, but it was not a dictatorial body, capable of acting arbitrarily and leaving its officers free to act without responsibility; it was itself to be under a code of laws of its own.

There soon arose, in addition to the Constitutions themselves, a body of statutes, general laws, edicts, opinions, rules and regulations enacted by Grand Lodges from year to year as needed, and by constitutional means. The distinction between those latter and the Constitutions, properly called, is that Constitutions create and define a Grand Lodge; the laws enacted by a Grand Lodge are its means of carrying on the work required of it by the Constitutions. The latter is operational law. Together, this whole body of law, constitutive and operational, is called "The Grand Lodge Code."

Each Grand Lodge has its own Code. They are alike in their principles but are unlike in their form and details. If a Grand Lodge wishes, it can print both its Constitution and its general laws in one volume; or it may print its Constitution in one book, its general laws in another; or it may print its Constitution in a single book, but leave its general laws uncollected, though on record in its Proceedings; or, yet again, it may publish the latter in the form of a Digest for reference purposes.

In any event, a Worshipful Master and his associate officers have that Code to guide them; not only to guide, but to govern them, because if an action taken by a Lodge violates the Code, that action is null and void, and when so it may lead to painful consequences—it may even lead to the withdrawal of a Lodge Charter. It is therefore surprising that Worshipful Masters often have never heard of their own Grand Lodge Code; at least, have not read it, and do not know that they themselves, and officially, are answerable to it. If that be true a Worshipful Master thus uninformed is working in the dark, and cannot be sure of himself in the government and guidance of his Lodge, especially if his plans chance to raise any question of Masonic law or of established and regular Masonic practice.

If a strict legal nomenclature were in force, the word "Constitution" would denote only that body of constitutive laws by which a Grand Lodge is created and by means of which it governs itself, and "Code" would denote the body of general laws, statutes, etc., which it enacts after it has been created; but for one reason or another the two are usually incorporated in the same book which is called "The Code." When that is done, however, the distinction is recognized in the body of the book by putting the Constitution at the beginning; sometimes preceded, or followed, by excerpts from the "Old Charges;" and named "Book of Constitutions," or "Constitutions of the Grand Lodge," or some similar title, with the remainder of the book called "Code of the Grand Lodge," "Statutes and General Laws," or by some other similar name.

Regardless of what plan is followed by his own Grand Lodge, any Worshipful Master can find the Book of Constitutions in its published laws, if not in a separate publication, then in the front of an omnibus publication. He can assume that the phraseology was one used either by the founders of his Grand Lodge or is as revised, or amended, by the Grand Lodge subsequently— (every Masonic Constitution provides means for its own amendment or for additions). He will therefore expect that in other Grand Jurisdictions the wording will not be the same as his own, that their versions will include some sections on topics not included in his own or exclude some sections that are; these differences in form and language do not matter because in substance and purpose Constitutions throughout America's forty-nine Grand Lodges are the same.

Since there are so many versions of the "Book of Constitutions" in the American Craft it is impossible to give an outline of each of them in a few pages; but it would not be necessary because they are so much alike. If three of them are compared, particularly if they represent the Grand Jurisdictions from one coast to the other, it will be sufficient. Those here chosen for that purpose are the Grand Lodges of New York, Iowa, and California. (These three would be representative on other grounds because in each one an extraordinary amount of Masonic legal scholarship has gone into the making of its Book of Constitutions.)

.A.

New York

The title of the Grand Lodge is "The Grand Lodge of Free and Accepted Masons of the State of New York." Sections 1 to 8 inclusive give the jurisdiction and composition of the Grand Lodge, name its elective and appointive officers, their titles, and define the duties of the Commission of Appeals and of the Judge Advocate.

Section 9 consists of six pages which define the composition and duties of the Trustees of the Hall and Asylum Fund which are in charge of the Masonic Hall, the Home and Hospital, Outside Relief, and Endowments.

Sections 10 to 16 state who may be elected Grand Master, when Grand Communications are to be held, and how Lodges are represented.

Sections 17 to 21 (inclusive) define the governmental powers of the Grand Lodge and of the Lodges under the heads of executive, legislative, and judicial, and state that these are under control of the Ancient Landmarks, the written Constitution, laws, usages, customs, etc.

Sections 22 to 30 (inclusive) describe the powers and duties of the Grand Officers in detail. (It is noticeable that in paragraph 14 of Section 22 the office of Grand Master is explicitly stated to possess "inherent" powers, implied in the Constitution itself but not named—this moot question bristles with difficulties).

Sections 31 to 33 (inclusive) describe the duties of District Deputy Grand Masters.

Sections 34 to 36 describe the duties of the Grand Lecturer and District Grand Lecturers and provide for a Standard Work.

Sections 37 to 38 provide for Grand Lodge revenues, with a schedule of fixed charges for dispensations, fees, etc.

Sections 39 to 78 define the formation, composition, powers, and duties of Lodges.

Sections 79 to 98 define Lodge membership, petition, initiation, balloting, affiliation, etc.

Sections 99 to 105 are concerned with Lodge jurisdiction, penal powers, and discipline, and amendments of the Grand Lodge Constitution.

The preceding materials are divided into four chapters. These are followed by a chapter on Definitions and by one on Rules of Order. The latter half of the volume, which is a small one, contains the Old Charges, the Grand Lodge Charter (the Grand Lodge was created by a written Charter issued by the Ancient Grand Lodge of England), the Acts of Incorporation (to comply with state law), Blank Forms, the Benevolent Orders Law of the State of New York, and Index.

.B.

IOWA

The volume entitled *Constitution and Code of the Grand Lodge of Iowa of Free and Accepted Masons* consists of the Ancient Constitutions (*Old Charges*), Constitution of the Grand Lodge of Iowa, and the Masonic Code of Iowa, divided into two parts. General Laws (sections 1 296 inclusive); and Trials, Punishments and Regulations (sections 297 to 432 inclusive); and Index.

The Constitution itself is much briefer than the Constitution of New York (it contains nineteen short articles); the more detailed definitions and provisions are carried over into the Code.

Article I. Name and style.

II. Of its [the Grand Lodge's] members and their qualifications.

III. Of the Powers and Authority of Grand Lodge.

IV. Of Communications [Grand Lodge].

V. Of Elections and Appointments.

VI. Of Vacancies—Offices and How Filled.

VII. Of Eligibility [to Grand Lodge Office].

VIII. Of Past Grand Officers.

IX. Of Voting.

X. Of the Powers and Duties of Officers.

XI. Of the Work [Ritual] of the Jurisdiction.

.C.

CALIFORNIA

*The Constitution of the M∴ W∴ Grand Lodge, F. &
A.M., of the Jurisdiction of California* is a volume of 455
pages, and includes the Monitorial Work, Ceremonies,
Old Charges, etc.

(A Constitution is a body of laws, comformable to the
Ancient Landmarks, which create a Grand Lodge and by
which it is governed. After the Grand Lodge is in existence, and in order to carry out the duties required of it
by its Constitution, it enacts what may be described as
General Laws. Thus, a provision for the existence of the
office of a Grand Master is a constitutional law because
that office is constitutive of a Grand Lodge; whereas a law
which grants him authority to have the assistance of District Deputy Grand Masters is not a constitutional law
because a Grand Lodge is whole and complete without a
District Deputy System, and it is therefore an administrative provision and belongs to some species of General
Laws. In its printed book of laws a Grand Lodge, as we
have seen, may print its constitutional law in a separate
body, consisting of sections or paragraphs, at the beginning
of the book, thereby setting it apart from the body of
General laws; the Grand Lodge of Iowa does this. Or a
Grand Lodge may incorporate in each provision of its

constitutional law the administrative machinery to implement it, but only in the form of a bare statement, leaving the more detailed administrative provisions to its General Laws; this method is employed by New York. Again, a Grand Lodge may not set its Constitutional provisions apart, in a separate body, but will incorporate with each of them in turn the General Laws which are the means to administer it, so that the Constitution and the General Laws comprise a single body of sections and paragraphs. This plan is followed by the Grand Lodge of California.)

PART I

Of the Organization of the Grand Lodge.

This Part contains nine Articles in 42 sections on Title, Members, Powers, Communications, Elections, Voting, Committees, Trustees, and Revenues.

PART II

Of the Grand Officers and Their Powers and Duties.

In seven Sections and 29 Articles covering the Grand Master, Deputy Grand Master and Wardens, Grand Treasurer, Grand Secretary, Grand Lecturer, Appointive Grand Officers, and their Expenses.

PART III

Of the Subordinate Lodges.

In four Articles and 63 Sections on Organization of a Lodge, Powers and Duties, Prohibitions, Dissolution of Lodges.

PART IV

Of the Officers of Subordinate Lodges.

In six Articles and 19 Sections on Elections, Master, Wardens, Treasurer, Secretary, and Appointed Officers.

PART V

Of Individual Masons.

In two Articles and 14 Sections on Membership of a Lodge and their Rights and Duties.

PART VI

Of Trials, Penalties, Appeals, and Restoration.

In five Articles and 48 Sections on Relation to Grand Masters, to Worshipful Masters, to Lodges, to Masons Individually, to Revisions and Reversals, and to Amendments, etc.

PART VII

Of Amendments, Definitions and Forms.

In three Articles and 46 Sections on Amendments, Definitions and Forms for Various Purposes.

Among the methods which he himself adopts to give his Lodge a peaceable, harmonious, and prosperous year it is wise for a Worshipful Master to place first among his plans one or two hours to familiarize himself with the general outline of his own Grand Lodge Code (to give it that title for the sake of convenience), because in it he will find his own duties specified and because it is the ground on which he must stand when he makes his own plans and decisions. There are a number of suggestions which he can ponder when so doing:

1. Secure a copy of the Code for your own private and continual use, and make sure that a Lodge copy is kept on the Secretary's desk.

2. Go through the Code from first to last, not to read every word or even every section, but to familiarize yourself with its general character and to fix in your mind an outline of the subjects covered by it.

3. Practice to learn how to find quickly any item in it by use of the Table of Contents and Index.

4. Search out every Section, Article, or Paragraph which provides for, or which involves, the office of Worshipful Master. (Some Masters separate those and have them typed in a pocket memorandum book.)

5. If a motion is made in Lodge, or if you are making plans of your own in which a question of law is involved, or about which it is possible that such a question could be raised, settle the question of law first, by consulting the Code, or, if that does not make it clear, by consulting your District Deputy (if you have one) or the Grand Master. Any action by a Master, or by the Lodge, which violates a law is forbidden, and that regardless of how wise or desirable it otherwise may be.

6. If a Master's decision or action is questioned in Lodge on grounds involving the law he is wise to clear that question at once by reading from the Code the article which applies to it, for while any Lodge may question a Master, no Lodge can question its own Grand Lodge law.

7. If, on the other hand, it is not the Lodge which questions an act of the Master but the Master who questions some motion or act of the Lodge, it is wisest to clear the issue, and in a manner to preserve a peaceable understanding, for him to quote the Code at the time.

8. Have a copy of the Code at hand when presiding over the Lodge, or when making decisions at other times, or when sitting with a Committee.

9. If a Master comes into the office with a vague or confused understanding of his duties, what he can or cannot do, ought or ought not to do, how much leeway he has for deciding things for himself, and how large is his scope for non-official activities inside or outside the Lodge room, he will find in his Code a resumé of a Master's powers and

a map of a Master's duties which, if he master it, will give him an assured and clear-cut understanding of himself as an Officer, and of his place and function in the Craft.

10. The Office of Master is not confined to the Master's own Lodge; he is a member of Grand Lodge and will have a voice and a vote in its Communications; and he has a place among officers of sister Lodges, for Masters must often work together. A Master can learn much about the Office during his years as Warden, and from within his own Lodge, but he can learn little there about comity among Lodges or his duties in and to Grand Lodge; it is in the Code that he best can learn these extra-Lodge duties.

CHAPTER IV

THE ANCIENT LANDMARKS

WHEN a Worshipful Master must take action concerning his Lodge, or must decide whether or not to approve some proposed Lodge activity, and is uncertain whether a given decision would be in keeping with the nature and purposes of Freemasonry, or is in harmony with its basic laws, he can find an infallible guide for himself in the Ancient Landmarks. No Landmark can be so stated as to decide such questions for him; he must frame his decision for himself; nevertheless he can form his decision on the basis of some Landmark, and if he does so he will be safe; even if his decision turns out in practice, or in results, to have been mistaken, it will be merely a mistake and will not lay him open to a charge of ignoring, or of intentionally violating, any Masonic law.

In any Lodge or Grand Lodge are a number of customs or practices which could be omitted without any change in what Freemasonry is; if, to give only one example, the wearing of formal dress by the officers is obligatory in a Lodge, an officer could not wear informal dress without violating a rule of his Lodge; nevertheless, it is obvious that the wearing of formal dress does not belong to the essence of Freemasonry—a Lodge without it is as wholly Masonic as one with it. The exact opposite is true of a Landmark. Freemasonry could not exist without it; to violate it is to act un-Masonically; if it were destroyed, the whole of Freemasonry would be destroyed along with it. If an example is needed, consider what the consequences would be if women were to be admitted to membership; immediately that were done, other fundamental changes would have to be made in consequence (preparation of the candidate would be one), and ultimately everything essential to Freemasonry would be altered. Similar consequences would follow if any other principle, rule, or practice having the power of a Landmark were omitted. The first of all obligations binding on a Master is the one that neither himself nor his Lodge shall ever violate or remove one of the Ancient Landmarks.

The Landmarks belong to that category of Masonic laws which is called "The Unwritten Law." There are laws of another kind in that same classification; those belonging to Etiquette are an example of them, for, though a Mason may be expelled for violating a law of Etiquette, no Grand Lodge has ever enacted a code of Etiquette in the form of written laws. The Landmarks are the first and the most important of the Unwritten Laws. A written law is such that it does not exist unless it is enacted in a written form; and, when it is enacted, the phrasing, or form of words, is essential to it. If a Grand Lodge, for example, enacts a law stating, "Each Lodge must pay annual Grand Lodge dues of one dollar per member," it is evident that if "each," or "Lodge," or "annual," or "one dollar" were to be omitted, the law would cease to exist. It is not so with the Unwritten Laws. They do not have to be enacted or written.

To say that a Landmark is not a Written Law is not, however, the same as to say that it cannot be described, or printed out, or named, or defined in written form. It can be, and often it is. What is meant is that a Landmark does not depend for its existence upon being written; and if it were written it would not consist of the form of words that were used. If a Landmark exists, it can be seen; if it can be seen, it can be thought out; if it can be thought out, it can be stated. It existed before the statement was made; it exists independently of the statement; it would continue to exist (unchanged) if the statement were destroyed; nevertheless, it is often useful to have such a statement.

Some Grand Lodges have never adopted any statement of the Landmarks, even for the sake of their usefulness; there is no reason, one way or another, why they should. Other Grand Lodges have adopted a statement of a few of them, perhaps only three or four, largely for the sake of keeping Lodges reminded of them. A few Grand Lodges have adopted a long list of statements, fifty-six in one case. But these lists, whether short or long, are statements only; no Grand Lodge can enact a Landmark; it can never identify a Landmark with any set form of words; and a Grand Lodge with a long list of statements cannot deny recognition to any other Regular Grand Lodge which has adopted none at all, yet all are governed by them.

The most famous and widely used of such statements is the list of twenty-five which Albert G. Mackey prepared, and which, in an elaborate form, he printed in Book I, Chapter 1, of his great work on *The Jurisprudence of Freemasonry*. About one-half of the American Grand Lodges have printed this list in their Codes; of these, one-half have adopted them officially; the other half have not expressed official opinion but print them for the sake of convenience. Mackey himself knew that a Landmark cannot be enacted by a Grand Lodge, nor can it be reduced to any form of words; he showed this by entitling his chapter: "The Landmarks, or The Unwritten Law." Nor would he have deemed the number "twenty-five" to be itself a Landmark; a list could include fewer than twenty-five, depending on taste, or on the method of classification that may be employed; but, in a long and practical experience in Masonic Jurisprudence, he had found these twenty-five to be a convenient number.

These explanations and provisos are set forth in order to protect a reader against misinterpreting the purpose of incorporating in this book Mackey's famous chapter, which will immediately follow. If a Worshipful Master's own Grand Lodge has never officially adopted Mackey's list or his statement of them, or even if it does not print the list in its own Proceedings, he will nevertheless find the chapter a convenient reference, and a safe guide in practice. The first three pages of the chapter, which contain a discussion of Mackey's theory of the Landmarks, are omitted:

LANDMARK FIRST

The Modes of Recognition are, of all the Landmarks, the most legitimate and unquestioned. They admit of no variation; and if ever they have suffered alteration or addition, the evil of such a violation of the ancient law has always made itself subsequently manifest. An admission of this is to be found in the proceedings of the Masonic Congress at Paris, where a proposition was presented to render these modes of recognition once more universal—a proposition which never would have been necessary, if the integrity of this important Landmark had been rigorously preserved.

LANDMARK SECOND

The Division of Symbolic Freemasonry Into Three Degrees, is a Landmark that has been better preserved than almost any other, although even here the mischievous spirit of innovation has left its traces, and by the disruption of its concluding portion from the Third Degree, a want of uniformity has been created in respect to the final teaching of the Master's order; and the Royal Arch of England, Scotland, Ireland, and America, and the "high degrees" of France and Germany, are all made to differ in the mode in which they lead the neophyte to the great consummation of all symbolic Freemasonry. In 1813, the Grand Lodge of England vindicated the ancient Landmark, by solemnly enacting that Ancient Craft Masonry consisted of the three degrees of Entered Apprentice, Fellow Craft, and Master Mason, *including the Holy Royal Arch*. But the disruption has never been healed, and the Landmark, although acknowledged in its integrity by all, still continues to be violated.

LANDMARK THIRD

The Legend of the Third Degree is an important Landmark, the integrity of which has been well preserved. There is no rite of Freemasonry, practiced in any country or language, in which the essential elements of this legend are not taught. The lectures may vary, and indeed are constantly changing, but the legend has ever remained substantially the same. And it is necessary that it should be so, for the legend of the Temple Builder constitutes the very essence and identity of Freemasonry. Any rite which excludes it, or materially alters it, would at once, by that exclusion or alteration, cease to be a Masonic rite.

LANDMARK FOURTH

The Government of the Fraternity, by a presiding officer called a Grand Master, who is elected from the body of the Craft, is a fourth Landmark of the Order. Many persons ignorantly suppose that the election of the Grand Master is held in consequence of a law or regulation of the Grand Lodge. Such, however, is not the case. The office is indebted for its existence to a Landmark of the

Order. Grand Masters are to be found in the records of the Institution long before Grand Lodges were established; and if the present system of legislative government by Grand Lodges were to be abolished, a Grand Master would still be necessary. In fact, although there has been a period within the records of history, and indeed of very recent date, when a Grand Lodge was unknown, there never has been a time when the Craft did not have their Grand Master.

LANDMARK FIFTH

The Prerogative of the Grand Master to Preside over every assembly of the Craft, wheresoever and whensoever held, is a fifth Landmark. It is in consequence of this law, derived from ancient usage, and not from any special enactment, that the Grand Master assumes the chair, or as it is called in England, "the throne," at every communication of the Grand Lodge; and that he is also entitled to preside at the Communication of every Subordinate Lodge, where he may happen to be present.

LANDMARK SIXTH

The Prerogative of the Grand Master to grant Dispensations for conferring degrees at irregular times, is another and a very important Landmark. The statutory law of Freemasonry requires a month, or other determinate period, to elapse between the presentation of a petition and the election of a candidate. But the Grand Master has the power to set aside or dispense with this probation, and to allow a candidate to be initiated at once. This prerogative he possessed in common with all Masters, before the enactment of the law, requiring a probation, and as no statute can impair his prerogative, he still retains the power, although the Masters do not.

LANDMARK SEVENTH

The Prerogative of the Grand Master to Give Dispensations for opening and holding Lodges is another Landmark. He may grant, in virtue of this, to a sufficient number of Freemasons, the privileges of meeting together and conferring degrees. The Lodges thus established are called "Lodges under Dispensation." They are strictly creatures of the Grand Master, created by his authority, existing only during his will and pleasure, and liable at any moment to be dissolved at his command. They may be continued for a day, a month, or indefinitely; but whatever be the period of their existence, they are indebted for that existence solely to the grace of the Grand Master.

LANDMARK EIGHTH

The Prerogative of the Grand Master to make Freemasons at Sight, is a Landmark which is closely connected with the preceding one. There has been much misapprehension in relation to this Landmark, which misapprehension has sometimes led to a denial of its existence in jurisdictions where the Grand Master was perhaps at the very time substantially exercising the prerogative, without the slightest remark or opposition. It is not to be supposed that the Grand Master can retire with a profane into a private room, and there, without assistance, confer the degrees of Freemasonry upon him. No such prerogative exists, and yet many believe that this is the so much talked of right of "making Masons at sight."

The real mode, and the only mode of exercising the prerogative, is this: The Grand Master summons to his assistance not less than six other Freemasons, convenes a Lodge, and without any previous probation, but on *sight* of the candidate, confers the degrees upon him, after which he dissolves the Lodge, and dismisses the brethren. Lodges thus convened for special purposes are called "Occasional Lodges." This is the only way in which any Grand Master within the records of the Institution has ever been known to legally "make a Mason at sight." The prerogative is dependent upon that of granting Dispensations to open and hold Lodges.

If the Grand Master has the power of granting to any other Mason the privilege of presiding over Lodges working by his Dispensation, he may assume this privilege of presiding—to himself; and as no one can deny his right to revoke his Dispensation granted to a number of brethren at a distance, and to dissolve the Lodge at his pleasure, it will scarcely be contended that he may not revoke his Dispensation for a Lodge over which he himself has been presiding, and dissolve the Lodge as soon as the business for which he had assembled it is accomplished. The making of Freemasons at sight is only the conferring of the degrees by the Grand Master, at once, in an Occasional Lodge, constituted by his dispensing power for the purpose, and over which he presides in person.

LANDMARK NINTH

The Necessity for Freemasons to Congregate in Lodges is another Landmark. It is not to be understood by this that any ancient Landmark has directed that permanent organization of subordinate Lodges which constitutes one of the features of the Masonic system as it now prevails. But the Landmarks of the Order always prescribed that Freemasons should from time to time congregate, for the purpose of either operative or speculative labor, and that these congregations should be called *Lodges*. Formerly these were temporary meetings called together for special purposes, and then dissolved, the brethren departing to meet again at other times and other places, according to the necessity of circumstances. But Warrants of Constitution, By-laws, permanent officers and annual meetings, are modern innovations wholly outside of the Landmarks, and dependent entirely on the special enactments of a comparatively recent period.

LANDMARK TENTH

The Government of the Craft, when so congregated in a Lodge by a Master and two Wardens, is also a Landmark. To show the influence of this ancient law, it may be observed by the way, that a congregation of Freemasons meeting together under any other government, as that for instance of a president and vice-president, or a chairman and sub-chairman, would not be recognized as a Lodge. The presence of a Master and two Wardens is as essential to the valid organization of a Lodge as a Warrant of Constitution is at the present day. The names, of course, vary in different languages, the Master, for instance, being called *Venerable* in French Freemasonry, and the Wardens *Surveillants,* but the officers, their number, prerogatives and duties, are everywhere identical.

LANDMARK ELEVENTH

The Necessity That Every Lodge, When Congregated, Should be Duly Tiled, is an important Landmark of the Institution, which is never neglected. The necessity of this law arises from the esoteric character of Freemasonry. As an Institution with secrets its portals must of course be guarded from the intrusion of the profane, and such a law must therefore always have been in force from the very beginning of the Order. It is therefore properly classed among the most ancient Landmarks. The office of Tiler is wholly independent of any special enactment of Grand

or Subordinate Lodges, although these may, and do, pre-
scribe for him additional duties, which vary in different
jurisdictions. But the duty of guarding the door, and
keeping off cowans and eavesdroppers, is an ancient one,
which constitutes a Landmark for his government.

LANDMARK TWELFTH

The Right Of Every Freemason To Be Represented in
all general meetings of the Craft, and to instruct his representatives, is a twelfth Landmark. Formerly, these general meetings, which were usually held once a year, were
called *General Assemblies,* and all the fraternity, even
to the youngest Entered Apprentice, were permitted to be
present. Now they are called *Grand Lodges,* and only the
Masters and Wardens of the Subordinate Lodges are summoned, though any Mason may attend if vouched for and
there is room for him. This is simply as the representatives
of their members. Originally, each Freemason represented
himself; now he is represented by his officers. This was a
concession granted by the fraternity about 1717, and of
course does not affect the integrity of the Landmark, for
the principle of representation is still preserved. The concession was only made for purposes of convenience.

LANDMARK THIRTEENTH

The Right Of Every Freemason To Appeal from the
decision of his brethren in Lodge convened, to the Grand
Lodge or General Assembly of Freemasons, is a Landmark
highly essential to the preservation of justice, and the
prevention of oppression. A few modern Grand Lodges,
in adopting a regulation that the decision of Subordinate
Lodges, in cases of expulsion, cannot be wholly set aside
upon an appeal, have violated this unquestioned Landmark, as well as the principles of just government.

LANDMARK FOURTEENTH

The Right Of Every Freemason To Visit and sit in every regular Lodge is an unquestionable Landmark of the Order. This is called *the right of visitation.* This right of visitation has always been recognized as an inherent right, which inures to every Freemason as he travels through the world. And this is because Lodges are justly considered as only divisions for convenience of the universal Masonic family. This right may, of course, be impaired or forfeited on special occasions by various circumstances; but when admission is refused to a Freemason in good standing, who knocks at the door of a Lodge as a visitor, it is to be expected that some good and sufficient reason shall be furnished for this violation, of what is in general a Masonic right, founded on the Landmarks of the Order.

LANDMARK FIFTEENTH

It is a Landmark of the Order, That No Visitor, Unknown To the Brethren Present, or to some one of them as a Freemason, can enter a Lodge without first passing an examination according to ancient usage. Of course, if the visitor is known to any brother present to be a Mason in good standing, and if that brother will vouch for his qualifications, the examination may be dispensed with, as the Landmark refers only to strangers, who are not to be recognized unless after strict trial, due examination, or lawful information.

LANDMARK SIXTEENTH

No Lodge Can Interfere In The Business Of Another Lodge, nor give degrees to brethren who are members of other Lodges. This is undoubtedly an ancient Landmark, founded on the great principles of courtesy and fraternal kindness, which are at the very foundation of our Institution. It has been repeatedly recognized by subsequent statutory enactments of all Grand Lodges.

LANDMARK SEVENTEENTH

It is a Landmark that Every Freemason Is Amenable To The Laws And Regulations Of The Masonic Jurisdiction in which he resides, and this although he may not be a member of any Lodge. Non-affiliation, which is, in fact, in itself a Masonic offence, does not exempt a Freemason from Masonic jurisdiction.

LANDMARK EIGHTEENTH

Certain Qualifications Of Candidates For Initiation are derived from a Landmark of the Order. These qualifications are that he shall be a man—shall be unmutilated, free born, and of mature age. That is to say, a woman, a cripple, or a slave, or one born in slavery, is disqualified for initiation into the rites of Freemasonry. Statutes, it is true, have from time to time been enacted, enforcing or explaining these principles; but the qualifications really arise from the very nature of the Masonic Institution, and from its symbolic teachings, and have always existed as Landmarks.

LANDMARK NINETEENTH

A Belief In The Existence Of God As The Grand Architect of the Universe, is one of the most important Landmarks of the Order. Always it has been deemed essential that a denial of the existence of a Supreme and Superintending Power, is an absolute disqualification for initiation. The annals of the Order never yet have furnished, or could furnish, an instance in which an avowed atheist was ever made a Freemason. The very initiatory ceremonies of the First Degree forbid and prevent the possibility of so monstrous an occurrence.

LANDMARK TWENTIETH

Subsidiary to this belief in God, as a Landmark of the Order, is The Belief In a Resurrection To A Future Life. This Landmark is not so positively impressed on the candidate by exact words as is the preceding Landmark; but the doctrine is taught by very plain implication, and runs through the whole symbolism of the Order. To believe in Freemasonry, and not to believe in a resurrection, would be an absurd anomaly, which could only be excused by the reflection, that he who thus confounded his belief and his skepticism, was so ignorant of the meaning of both theories as to have no rational foundation for his knowledge of either.

LANDMARK TWENTY-FIRST

It is a Landmark, that a "Book Of The Law" shall constitute an indispensable part of the furniture of every Lodge. I say advisedly, a *Book of the Law,* because it is not absolutely required that everywhere the Old and New Testaments shall be used. The "Book of the Law" is that volume which, by the religion of the country, is believed by the candidate to contain the revealed will of the Grand Architect of the Universe. Hence, in all Lodges in Christian countries, the Book of the Law is composed of the Old and New Testaments; in a country where Judaism was the prevailing faith, the Old Testament alone would be sufficient; and in Mohammedan countries, and among Mohammedan Freemasons, the Koran might be substituted. Freemasonry does not attempt to interfere with the peculiar religious faith of its disciples, except in so far as it relates to the belief in the existence of God, and what necessarily results from that belief. The Book of the Law is to the Speculative Freemason his spiritual Trestle-board, without this he cannot labor; whatever he believes to be the revealed will of the Grand Architect constitutes for him this spiritual Trestle-board, and must ever be before him in his hours of speculative labor, to be the rule and guide of his conduct. The Landmark, therefore, requires that a Book of the Law, a religious code of some kind, purporting to be an exemplar of the revealed will of God, shall form an essential part of the furniture of every Lodge.

LANDMARK TWENTY-SECOND

The Equality Of All Masons is another Landmark of the Order. This equality has no reference to any sub-version of those gradations of rank which have been insti-tuted by the usage of society. The monarch, the nobleman or the gentleman is entitled to all the influence, and re-ceives all the respect which rightly belong to his exalted position. But the doctrine of Masonic equality implies that, as children of one great Father, we meet in the Lodge upon the level—that on that level we are all traveling to one predestined goal—that in the Lodge genuine merit shall receive more respect than wealth, and that virtue and knowledge alone should be the basis of all Masonic honors, and be rewarded with preferment. When the labors of the Lodge are over, and the brethren have retired from their peaceful retreat, to mingle once more with the world, each will then again resume that social position, and exercise the privileges of that rank, to which the customs of society entitle him.

LANDMARK TWENTY-THIRD

The Secrecy Of The Institution is another and a most important Landmark. There is some difficulty in precisely defining what is meant by a *secret society*. If the term refers, as perhaps, in strictly logical language it should, to those associations whose designs are concealed from the public eye, and whose members are unknown, which produce their results in darkness, and whose operations are carefully hidden from the public gaze—a definition which will be appropriate to many political clubs and revolutionary combinations in despotic countries, where reform, if it is to be effected at all, must be effected by stealth—then clearly Freemasonry is not a secret society.

Its design is not only publicly proclaimed, but is vaunted by its disciples as something to be venerated—its disciples are known, for its membership is considered an honor to be coveted—it works for a result of which it boasts—the civilization and refinement of man, the amelioration of his condition, and the reformation of his manners.

But if by a secret society is meant—and this is the most correct understanding of the term—a society in which there is a certain amount of knowledge, whether it be of methods of recognition, or of legendary and traditional learning, which is imparted only to those who have passed through an established form of initiation, the form itself being also concealed or esoteric, then in this sense is Freemasonry undoubtedly a secret society. Now this form of secrecy is a form inherent in it, existing with it from its very foundation, and secured to it by its ancient Landmarks. If divested of its secret character, it would lose its identity, and would cease to be Freemasonry.

Whatever objections may, therefore, be made to the Institution, on account of its secrecy, and however much some unskillful brethren may have been willing in times of trial, for the sake of expediency, to divest it of its secret character, it will ever be impossible to do so, even were the Landmark not standing before us as an insurmountable obstacle; because such change of its character would be social suicide, and the death of the Order would follow its legalized exposure. Freemasonry, as a secret association, has lived unchanged for centuries—as an open society it would not last for as many years.

LANDMARK TWENTY-FOURTH

The Foundation Of A Speculative Science Upon an Operative Art, and the symbolic use and explanation of the terms of that art, for purposes of religious or moral teaching, constitute another Landmark of the Order. The Temple of Solomon was the symbolic cradle of the Institution, and, therefore, the reference to the operative Masonry, which constructed that magnificent edifice, to the materials and implements which were employed in its construction, and to the artists who were engaged in the building, are all component and essential parts of the body of Freemasonry, which could not be subtracted from it without an entire destruction of the whole identity of the Order. Hence, all the comparatively modern rites of Freemasonry, however they may differ in other respects, religiously preserve this temple history and these operative elements, as the substratum of all their modifications of the Masonic system.

LANDMARK TWENTY-FIFTH

The last and crowning Landmark of all is, that These Landmarks Can Never Be Changed. Nothing can be subtracted from them—nothing can be added to them—not the slightest modification can be made in them. As they were received from our predecessors, we are bound by the most solemn obligations of duty to transmit them to our successors. Not one jot or one tittle of these unwritten laws can be repealed; for in respect to them, we are not only willing, but compelled to adopt the language of the sturdy old barons of England, *Nolumus leges mutari,* let the laws abide.

CHAPTER V

MASONIC JURISPRUDENCE

MASONIC Jurisprudence is not something which Freemasonry *has* but something which it *is*. Freemasonry is fellowship, symbolism, a system of teachings, a fraternity in Brotherly Love, Relief and Truth, ritualism, and many things besides. It also is a Lodge organization, Landmarks, offices, laws, rules, regulations, duties, prerogatives, rights, and privileges, and insofar as it is these latter things, it is a Jurisprudence; for this reason it is often said that the Fraternity does not look outside itself for government but *is* government; and that when its Jurisprudence is practiced, it is Masonry that is practiced. Its Jurisprudence therefore is nowhere wholly codified, nor does it exist in one place, but is here and there throughout the Craft; is not gathered together into any one office or single governing body; some of it is written and some is unwritten, some of it is in one office and some in other offices, some of it consists of laws or rules enacted and written down, and some of it consists of customs and procedures, principles, ideals, and traditions never written down.

When therefore a man learns Masonry by his practice and work in it, part of what he thus learns is Jurisprudence; when he signs his Petition, submits to the ordeal of the Ballot, takes his Degrees, joins a Lodge, has a voice and vote in a Lodge Communication, pays his dues, occupies an office and discharges the duties belonging to it, he is practicing Masonic Jurisprudence and therefore learns what it is while he is learning what Masonry is. In civil life we have congresses, assemblies, councils, and parliaments composed of men elected to their places, most of whom receive salaries and many of whom make a profession of their work in these bodies which enact our laws and ordinances. We have city, state, and federal courts; a profession consisting of lawyers who must spend years in college learning the laws and their technicalities; and, in addition, we have tens of thousands of offices and officers who enforce the law. This civil law applies to actions and to properties of a certain kind only; over others it has no jurisdiction; owing to this fact and to the separate organizations of law-making and law-enforcing bodies we tend to think of our national jurisprudence as something independent and apart, and of men who make and enforce the laws as a class or profession. But there is no such system as that in Freemasonry, and very little that is even remotely comparable with it, for we do not have separate Masonic legislatures, or a separate class of law enforcement officers, or a Masonic police force. Grand Lodges and Lodges act as legislative assemblies and as courts, but neither one of them is a body formed expressly for that purpose, and each of them is composed of Masons who occupy a place in these assemblies, not because he has been set aside to be a lawmaker, but because he is a member or an officer of the Lodge or the Grand Lodge.

Certain of our laws are written down, and others are not; certain of them are in the form of enactments by a Grand Lodge or a Lodge, and others consist of actions, customs, and traditions which each Mason learns as he goes along, and which even the officers do not learn in a law school but learn from the duties of their offices. It is a law, for example, that to enter a Lodge a Mason must don an Apron, knock on the door, and salute at the altar, but a Mason seldom thinks of it as being a law because to him it is one of those normal and familiar practices which belong to Masonry and help to make it what it is. The majority of Grand Lodge laws are nothing other than descriptions of what Lodges always have been and always have done; the only reason for enacting them in written form is to make sure that no Lodge breaks away from the ancient customs. The Ancient Landmarks themselves are only another name for various things that Lodges and Masons do, and have ever done, and unless every Lodge and Lodge member does them, Masonry ceases to be Masonry. It is therefore not as if our Jurisprudence were in a few books somewhere on a shelf which only the technically trained can understand, and which only certain officers ever have need of; it is only another name for Freemasonry itself insofar as certain things in the practice of it must, and shall be done, and in a certain way, without exception, and with no Mason excepted.

The need to know and practice jurisprudence is for this reason of a piece with every Mason's need to know and to understand Freemasonry in general. The member who sits on the side-lines already knows something of that jurisprudence as it applies to him as a member, and he learned it during the course of his Initiation and is learning more and more of it as he continues to take a part in Lodge Communications; but there is much in it which he cannot learn for himself, and where he sits. An officer knows much of the jurisprudence which applies to his own office because he has learned to practice his duties and has conned by heart the words which belong to his part; yet there are many other offices and stations and places, and often he needs to know and understand the duties and functions which belong to them because otherwise he will not be able to work in co-operation with them.

That in Freemasonry which constitutes jurisprudence cannot be carved out, set apart, and made over into something independent; it does not follow from this however that those elements in the Craft which belong to law and rule cannot be marked out for separate study. Masonic history also belongs to the Fraternity in the same way, is "bone of its bone, flesh of its flesh," so that Freemasonry is a living and embodied history, and that to such an extent that what it is cannot be separated off from the history of what it was; nevertheless Masonic history is a separate subject for study; has a place of its own, and a literature of its own. The same is true of Ritualism, Symbolism, Masonic Offices, Etiquette, and Parliamentary Law, each of which is marked off into a field of its own in which Masons make special studies and about which they have published several literatures.

Masonic jurisprudence is a magnificent subject, of which no man can know too much and any man seldom knows enough; if a Mason devotes himself to it, as his specialty in Craft service, he will discover it to be inexhaustible, and its importance will grow upon him endlessly, nor will he ever encounter any other specialized service of greater usefulness to his Brethren. His study will include such subjects as these: the nature and form of a Grand Lodge, its offices, and its powers. The nature of a Lodge, its functions, jurisdiction, officers, and its Rules of Order. The internal and external qualifications of Candidates, Petition, Balloting, Rejection, Examination. The duties, rights, and privileges of Entered Apprentices, Fellows of the Craft, Master Masons, unaffiliated Masons, visitors, sojourners. The nature of Masonic Crimes, what punishments are, trials, penal jurisdiction, restoration, and general discipline. Underlying the subject as a whole are the

Ancient Landmarks, those unwritten principles and practices which constitute Freemasonry's identity, and without which it would cease to exist; and along with the Landmarks that fundamental Body of Law consisting of the Book of Constitution, the *Old Charges,* the statutes, and such other Grand Lodge law as, with them, is designed for the government of the Fraternity as a whole in a given State or Country. The subject matter belonging to these heads is found partly in an analysis of the Craft as it is at work, and partly in Grand Lodge printed Codes, Grand Lodge Proceedings, and in Lodge By-Laws.

When in 1717 in London, England, the first Grand Lodge of Speculative Freemasonry was erected, it was formed by representatives of four or more old Lodges which had been at work for generations. The members of those Lodges had worked partly according to some old documents which they possessed, and partly according to a number of Landmarks, customs, and traditions which had come down orally. After the Grand Lodge was erected new Lodges began to be formed, and in the course of a few years their number began to increase rapidly; these "new men," unlike the members of the "old Lodges," were not familiar with Craft rules and traditions. Also, as the Craft became wholly Speculative, certain changes were made in the organization of the Lodges, new officers were added, new customs introduced. In consequence of these developments there came a demand for printed guidance; to satisfy that demand the Grand Lodge appointed a Committee, with Reverend James Anderson as its Chairman, and instructed it to prepare a Constitution in writing. This Constitution was submitted to the Grand Lodge for its approval, and in 1723 it was published and began to be distributed among the Lodges. A revised and enlarged edition of it was published in 1738.

The documents possessed by the "Old Lodges" before 1717 were of a number of types: *Old Charges,* Old Manuscripts, Old Constitutions, Catechisms, Ancient Manuscripts, etc., and, in addition, each Lodge had archives of its own such as Rolls, By-Laws, etc. The Anderson Committee had been instructed to collect as many of these as it could find and to collate and organize them so that, instead of a number of scattered documents, the Craft could have one book. When that book came into general circulation it was called the "Book of Constitutions" (an edition printed by Benjamin Franklin in 1734 was the first Masonic book ever published in America). As each new Grand Lodge was formed it organized itself according to that same Book; and though since then Grand Lodges have amended it, enlarged it, rewritten it, and have added to it a number of new Regulations and laws, it continues now to be everywhere the constitutional foundation of regular Grand Lodges; versions of either, or both, of the original editions of 1723 or 1738 are usually printed in the first part of Grand Lodge Codes for every Mason to read. If a Worshipful Master will read it and reread it, it will give him a clear knowledge of that in Masonic law which is as old as Masonry, and which lies at the root of the laws and rules made since it was first printed.

By the middle of the Nineteenth Century when Lodges had begun to multiply by thousands, when each State had come to have a law-making Body of its own in the form of a Grand Lodge, and when the Royal Arch, Cryptic Masonry, Templarism, and the Scottish Rite had become established as integral parts of the Fraternity, the slender Book of Constitutions was expanded into thick Grand Lodge Codes, a mass of new statutes, laws, rules, and regulations began to grow, and has continued to grow in each and every State, and Lodges in turn added one new ordinance after another to their by-laws as their own activities increased and became more diversified; in consequence Masonic law became too large a subject for any one Mason to carry about in his memory. Lodge and Grand Lodge Officers, and Worshipful Masters in particular, found themselves in need of hand-books of Masonic law, compendiums in which hundreds of laws and rules could be condensed into convenient form, and with explanations of the general principles underlying the laws of every kind and Rite. It was to satisfy that need that a number of learned Masons began to publish, one after another, treatises and volumes on jurisprudence, among them being such men as Mackey, Lockwood, Lawrence, Look, Cushing, Morris, Drummond, Engels, Pound, etc.

If by a classic is meant a book which comes into the widest possible use, which continues in such use generation after generation, and is accepted as a norm or standard for other books, the chief classic among works on Masonic Jurisprudence is *The Jurisprudence of Freemasonry,* by Albert G. Mackey. Mackey was a learned man outside of Freemasonry; in Freemasonry itself he was the most learned man in his century; the work of preparing his *Encyclopaedia* gave him a knowledge of the Fraternity over the world, throughout its history, under all its forms, and in every detail—which continues to be unrivalled; he had a continuous practical experience in the offices of Local and Grand Bodies in each and every Rite; he had a thorough knowledge of American Masonry in its ramifications at first-hand from much traveling and from a world-wide correspondence; was in communication, or in personal friendship, with scores of other Masonic scholars; and in addition had a grasp of Freemasonry as a whole which gave him perspective, and a just sense of the value of details. The result was a work which has not the status

7. The Prerogative of the Grand Master to Grant Dispensations for Opening and Holding Lodges.

8. The Prerogative of the Grand Master to Make Masons at Sight.

9. The Necessity for Freemasons to Congregate in Lodges.

10. The Government of the Craft, when so Congregated in a Lodge, by a Master and two Wardens.

11. The Necessity that Every Lodge, when Congregated, should be duly Tiled.

12. The Right of Every Freemason to be Represented in All General Meetings of the Craft.

13. The Right of Every Freemason to Appeal.

14. The Right of Every Freemason to Visit.

15. Unless Vouched For, a Visitor Must be Examined.

16. No Lodge Can Interfere in the Business of Another Lodge.

17. Every Freemason is Amenable to the Laws and Regulations.

18. Qualifications of Candidates.

19. A Belief in the Existence of God.

20. Belief in a Resurrection to a Future Life.

21. A "Book of the Law."

22. The Equality of All Masons.

23. The Secrecy of the Institution.

24. The Foundation of a Speculative Science upon an Operative Art.

25. The Landmarks Can Never be Changed.

Chapter II.   The Written Law.

These are "the Regulations" which "have been enacted from time to time by General Assemblies, Grand Lodges," etc. The Code of Written Law traces its origins to:

1. The Old York Constitution of 926 A.D., with its Fifteen Articles, and Fifteen Points.
2. The Constitution of Edward III.
3. Regulations of 1663.
4. The Ancient Installation Charges.
5. The Ancient Charges at Making.
6. The Regulation of 1703.
7. The Regulation of 1717.
8. The Regulation of 1720.
9. The Charges Approved in 1722 (included in the Anderson Constitution).
10. The General Regulations of 1721.

Book II. Law Relating to Candidates.

Chapter I. The Qualification of Candidates.

Section I. The Internal Qualifications.
1. Candidate must come of his own free will and accord.
2. He must be uninfluenced by mercenary motives.

Section II. The External Qualifications.
1. The Moral Qualifications.
   (a) Candidates must be under the tongue of good report.
   (b) They must believe in God.
   (c) Believe in a Future Life.
2. The Physical Qualifications.
   (a) The Candidate must be of the male sex.
   (b) He must be of legal age.
   (c) He must be hale and sound.
3. Mental Qualifications.
   (a) A candidate must be a lover of the Liberal Arts and Sciences.
   (b) Idiots and madmen are excluded.

4. Political Qualifications.
   (a) The candidate must be a free man.

Chapter II. The Petitions of Candidates.

1. A Candidate must apply by a written petition.
2. It must be signed by himself.
3. The Petitioner must be recommended by at least two members.
4. Application must be made to the Lodge nearest to Petitioner's place of residence except where jurisdiction is concurrent.
5. The Petition must be read on a regular night of meeting.
6. The Petition, having been once read, cannot be withdrawn.
7. The Petition must be referred to a Committee.
8. Once submitted, the Petition, if reported on, is acted on at the next regular meeting of the Lodge.
9. If the Committee reports unfavorably, the Candidate is rejected without Ballot because, presumably, the members of the Committee would black ball him. Some jurisdictions insist on Ballot.

Chapter III. Balloting for Candidates.

1. If a Petition is approved it is then submitted to Ballot.
2. The Ballot must be unanimous.
3. It is independent.
4. It is secret.
5. In event of an inadvertent error the Master alone has power to order another Ballot.

Chapter IV. Consequences of Rejection.

1. A Petition cannot be reconsidered by a vote.

2. The Petitioner can apply to no other Lodge for a definite period of time.

3. After the legal interval, a rejected Petitioner can apply for a second time to the same Lodge, or to another Lodge, but must state his previous rejection.

Book III.   Law Relating to Individual Freemasons.

Chapter I.   Of Entered Apprentices.

1. According to ancient rules, they are not entitled to Masonic Burial, or to Masonic Relief.

2. They can sit only in a Lodge of Entered Apprentices.

3. Can Petition for advancement to a higher Degree. (a) A Lodge has the right to reject such a Petition.

4. They should have ample time between Degrees to become proficient.

5. They are advanced by unanimous Ballot unless only one Ballot required for all three degrees.

6. They may apply at any Regular Communication for advancement.

7. They may forfeit their rights by un-Masonic conduct.

Chapter II.   Of Fellow Crafts.

1. Their rights and duties correspond to those of an Entered Apprentice in so far as they apply to a Lodge of Fellow Crafts.

Chapter III.   Of Master Masons.

1. A Master Mason has nine rights:
(a) The Right of Membership. (b) Of Affiliation. (c) Of Visit. (d) Of Avouchment. (e) Of Relief. (f) Of Demission. (g) Of Appeal. (h) Of Burial. (i) Of Trial.

Chapter IV. Of Past Masters.

1. This chapter applies to a Past Master of a Lodge.
2. In some Grand Jurisdictions they sit and vote in Grand Lodge.
3. They may, by courtesy, preside over the Lodge in the absence of the Worshipful Master, or at his or a Warden's request.
4. A Past Master may install his successor.
5. He is eligible to re-election as Master without having occupied the South and West a second time.
6. May by courtesy have a seat in the East.

Chapter V. Of unaffiliated Masons.

1. An unaffiliated Freemason is one who does not hold membership in any Lodge.
2. "Every Brother ought to belong to a Lodge."
3. (a) Every Unaffiliated Mason is still a member of the Fraternity at large and has obligations to it.
   (b) He is divested of all prerogatives which belong to him as a Lodge member.
4. He has a right to call for assistance when in imminent peril.
5. He has no right to pecuniary aid from a Lodge.
6. He cannot visit Lodges, or walk in Masonic processions.
7. He has no right to Masonic burial.
8. May be tried by the Lodge in whose jurisdiction he resides.
9. Persistent and perverse continuance as an unaffiliate is a violation of law, and such a Mason may be tried and expelled only by a trial and vote by his own lodge but this is seldom done.

Book IV. Law Relating to Lodges.

Chapter I. The Nature of a Lodge.

1. A petition for a Dispensation to form a new Lodge must satisfy seven conditions: (a) At least seven signers. (b) Each signer a Master Mason. (c) Each signer in good standing. (d) A good reason for a Lodge at that time and place. (e) Place of meeting designated. (f) Names of the three principal Officers must be designated. (g) It must be recommended by adjacent Lodges.

A Lodge at this stage is called an "inchoate Lodge."

2. After a certain interval the Grand Lodge issues a Charter, or Warrant.

3. The Charter is followed by four steps:
   a. Consecration.
   b. Dedication.
   c. Constitution.
   d. Installation.

Chapter II. The Rights of Subordinate Lodges.

1. Of Lodges Under Dispensation
   (a) Cannot be represented in Grand Lodge.
   (b) Cannot make By-Laws.
   (c) Cannot elect Officers.
   (d) Cannot therefore install Officers.
   (e) Cannot elect members.
   (f) Can elect Candidates.
2. Powers of Lodge Under a Charter.
   1. A Lodge has the right:
      (a) To retain possession of its Charter.
      (b) To do all the work of ancient Craft Masonry.
      (c) To transact Lodge business.

(d) To be represented in Grand Lodge.

(e) To admit new members.

(f) To elect officers.

(g) To install officers.

(h) To exclude a member.

(i) To make By-laws.

(j) To levy a tax on its members.

(k) To appeal to the Grand Lodge from decision of its Master.

(l) To exercise penal jurisdiction over its members.

(m) To select a name for itself, unless one is designated by Grand Lodge.

(n) To select time and place of its meetings.

Chapter III. The Officers of a Lodge.

1. The Officers usually to be found in American Lodges are as follows:

a.	Worshipful Master	f.	Senior Deacon
b.	Senior Warden	g.	Junior Deacon
c.	Junior Warden	h.	Two Stewards, Senior &
d.	Treasurer		Junior
e.	Secretary	i.	Tiler

2. These Officers are elected or appointed annually.

3. Traditionally, the Masonic year begins on December 27th, St. John the Evangelist's Day.

4. The Installation should follow as soon as possible after election.

Section I. The Worshipful Master. His duties and prerogatives are:

1. To preside over the Lodge.

2. He, and possibly with one or both of the Wardens, represents his Lodge in Grand Lodge.

3. He controls the admittance of visitors.

4. He may refuse to admit a Lodge member.

5. He has custody of the lodge Charter.

6. He has appointive powers.

7. He has one vote, and a casting vote if there be a tie.

8. He is not eligible to hold office of Master if he has not served as a Warden.

9. He is eligible to re-election.

10. He must have received the Past Master's Degree before installation.

11. The Grand Lodge alone has penal jurisdiction over him while in office.

Section II.   The Wardens.

1. The duties of the Senior Warden are, in the absence of the Worshipful Master, to preside over the Lodge; in his presence, to assist him in government of it.

2. If both the Master and Senior Warden are absent, the Junior Warden may preside, or he may ask a Past Master to do so and keep his own station; he appoints officers pro tem to fill in; if only the Senior Warden is absent the Junior Warden keeps his own station, and the Master appoints a Senior Warden; if only the Junior Warden is absent the Master appoints one.

3. Wardens may join the Master in representing the Lodge in Grand Lodge.

4. Wardens are eligible to election to the office of Master.

Section III.   The Treasurer.

1. He is to receive all monies due the Lodge from the Secretary.

2. He is to make due entries of the same.

3. He is to pay them out at order of the Master, and with consent of the Lodge.

Section IV. The Secretary.

1. He is the Lodge's recording, corresponding, and collecting agent.

Section V. The Deacons.

1.—The Senior Deacon is the special attendant of the Master.

2. The Junior Deacon is the special attendant of the Senior Warden.

Section VI. The Stewards.

1. Their principal duty is the preparation of Candidates.

2. Their traditional duty is to prepare the banquets, etc., and over a long period in Masonic history they had the duty of examining visitors.

Section VII. The Tiler.

1. He guards the Outer Door.

2. He prepares the Lodge for its meetings.

3. He need not be a member of the Lodge he tiles.

4. The Tiler is sometimes appointed by the Master, but more often is elected by the Lodge.

Section VIII. The Chaplain.

1. In the traditional usages of the Craft the Master performs all sacerdotal functions; therefore a Chaplain, if a Lodge have one, functions as an assistant to the Master.

Chapter IX   Rules of Order.

The Rules of Order consist of

    A. The Order of Business.

    B. Rules of Debate.

    C. Committees, the Constitution, appointment, duties.

    D. The manner of holding elections.

Book V. Law Relating to Grand Lodges.

Chapter I. The Nature of a Grand Lodge.

1. A Grand Lodge may be formed by not less than three Lodges in territory not already under jurisdiction of a Grand Lodge.

2. Immediately it is organized it issues Charters to its constituent Lodges.

3. It has exclusive jurisdiction in the United States and Canada over its Lodges and its territory.

Chapter II.

1. The functions of a Grand Lodge are in three classes: Legislative, Judicial, Executive.

Section 1. The Legislative Powers of a Grand Lodge.

1. It can make no regulation in violation of a Landmark.

2. Its legislation must be prospective, not retrospective.

3. It cannot repeal or alter a regulation except in the mode it has provided.

4. It can make by-laws for subordinate Lodges.

5. It grants Warrants, Charters, Dispensations.

6. It can revoke them.

7. It has taxing power.

Section 2. The Judicial Powers.

1. A Grand Lodge has both original and appellate jurisdiction.

2. It has original jurisdiction except where it has divested itself of that prerogative.

3. It may exercise jurisdiction in its own assemblies or by means of committees.

Section 3. Executive Powers.

1. The Grand Lodge has the power to put its own

enactments into effect, and to see that its laws are duly enforced.

2.   When not in Grand or Special Communications a Grand Lodge's executive powers reside in the office of Grand Master.

Chapter III.   Officers of a Grand Lodge.

Section I.   The Grand Master.

1.   He has the right to convene the Grand Lodge.

2.   He has the right to preside over every assembly of the Craft.

3.   He may visit any Masonic Lodge or assembly in his Jurisdiction.

4.   He has the right of appointment.

5.   He can cast a deciding vote in case of a tie.

6.   He can grant Dispensations.

7.   He can authorize the formation of a Lodge.

8.   He can make Freemasons at Sight.

Section II.   The Deputy Grand Master.

1.   He performs many of the functions of the Grand Master in the latter's absence.

Section III.   The Grand Wardens.

1.   Their duties are analogous to those of Lodge Wardens.

Section IV.   The Grand Treasurer.

1.   His duties are analogous to those of the Treasurer of a Lodge.

Section V.   The Grand Secretary.

1.   He records all Proceedings of the Grand Lodge.

2.   He conducts its correspondence.

3.   He receives Grand Lodge dues and returns.

4.   He is keeper of the Grand Lodge Seal.

Section VI.   The Grand Chaplain.

1.   He offers prayers at Grand Communications, and

conducts its devotional exercises on public occasions.

Section VII.   The Grand Lecturer.

    1.   He is the recognized teacher of the Ritual.

    2.   His appointment should be permanent.

    3.   The Grand Lecturer should have control and authority over any assistant Lecturers.

Section VIII.   The Grand Deacons.

    1.   Their duties are analogous to those of the Senior and Junior Deacons in Lodges.

Section IX.   The Grand Marshal.

    1.   He arranges the processions of Grand Lodge, and preserves order according to the forms prescribed.

Section X.   The Grand Pursuivant.

    1.   He is in charge of Grand Lodge regalia and insignia.

Section XI.   The Grand Sword Bearer.

    1.   He carries the Sword of State.

Section XII.   The Grand Stewards.

    1.   Their duties are analogous to those of Lodge Stewards.

Section XIII.   The Grand Tiler.

    1.   Duties are analogous to Lodge Tiler.

Section XIV.   Committee of Foreign Correspondence.

    1.   It reviews Proceedings of Grand Lodges which are recognized by its own Grand Lodge.

Book VI.   *Masonic Crimes and Punishments.*

Chapter I.   Masonic Crimes.

    1.   They are in three classes:

        A.   Violations of the Moral law.

        B.   Transgressions of the municipal law.

            (a)   The conviction of a man in civil court does not of itself affect a Mason's standing.

C. Violation of the Landmarks and Regulations. Among these are:
   (a) Disclosure of secrets.
   (b) Disobedience and want of respect for superior officers.
   (c) Private quarrels among Masons.
   (d) Discourtesy to other Masons.
   (e) Striking another Freemason except in self-defense.
   (f) Dishonoring wife or daughter of a Mason.
   (g) Gambling on Masonic premises. Etc., etc.

Chapter II. Masonic Punishments

Section I. Masonic Censure.

(a) A Lodge may move a vote or resolution to censure any member.

Section II. Reprimand.

(a) Reprimand must be preceded by charges and a trial.

(b) It may be administered in private, or in public.

(c) The Master is the proper officer to administer a reprimand.

(d) A reprimand does not affect Masonic standing.

Section III. Exclusion.

1. Temporary Exclusion. The Lodge by vote, or the Master on his own authority, may exclude a member from the Lodge during that Communication.

2. Permanent Exclusion.

Section IV. Suspension.

(a) Definite suspension is a deprivation of a member's rights and privileges for a fixed period of time.

(b) Indefinite Suspension is for no fixed time but is at the pleasure of the Lodge.

Section V. Expulsion.

1. Expulsion terminates a man's connection with the Fraternity in every particular except his duties under his obligations which continue in force.

2. The penalty is not inflicted so much as a punishment of the guilty person, as it is a safeguard for the security of the Order.

Chapter III. Restoration.

1. Restoration, or re-instatement, may be effected by either of two processes:

(a) By an act of clemency on the part of the Lodge, or the Grand Lodge.

(b) By a reversal of the sentence of the Lodge by the Grand Lodge.

Chapter IV. Penal Jurisdiction.

1. The geographical jurisdiction of a Lodge consists of the territory which belongs to it.

2. The personal jurisdiction of a Lodge is that penal jurisdiction which it exercises over its own members, wherever they may be situated.

(a) A Lodge exercises penal jurisdiction over all its members.

(b) Over all affiliated Masons not its members but in its geographical jurisdiction.

(c) Over non-affiliated Masons in its jurisdiction.

Chapter V. Masonic Trials.

1. The first step in a Masonic trial is the charge, which must be in writing, and made and filed in due time and form.

2. If the accused is living outside the Lodge's geographical jurisdiction the charges may be mailed to him.

3. The trial must commence at a regular Lodge Communication but may continue at a fixed time and elsewhere.

4. The Lodge must be Opened in the highest Degree to which the accuser has attained.

5. The rendering of the verdict must be made in Lodge.

6. It is a general rule that lodge visitors are excluded from a trial.

7. The testimony of Master Masons is usualy taken on their honor, as such.

8. The testimony of profanes may be taken in Committee.

9. At conclusion of the trial the accuser and accused retire when the question of guilt is voted upon.

10. If the verdict is guilty the Master then puts the question as to what punishment is to be inflicted, voting on the severest penalty first and, in decreasing severity, expulsion, suspension or reprimand.

The Jurisprudence of Freemasonry, by Albert G. Mackey, of which the above summary is little more than a table of contents, was written a century ago, before there was a literature on the subject, and at a time when the American Masonic System had not yet crystallized; it is not to be wondered at, therefore, that in spite of Dr. Mackey's thoroughness and caution, it is incomplete in the scope of the topics it discusses, or that modern Masonic practice has, in respect of some topics, moved in directions he could not have expected. Masonic Jurisprudence is organic and alive, grows and changes with the Fraternity, and no final or permanently complete review of it will ever be published; if therefore a few topics are here added which were not discussed by Mackey, it is not to complete his survey but rather to include such subjects as have been brought to the front in Jurisprudence since his day:

Mackey's Jurisprudence is kept up to date by frequent revisions.

1. Masonic Comity. This includes the rules and regulations which govern Grand Lodge relations among themselves and with other Masonic Bodies, and includes the great and vitally important topic of Grand Lodge Recognition; it falls into two general categories:

A.   Inter-Grand Lodge and Inter-Grand Jurisdictional affairs.

B.   A Grand Lodge's relations with Masonic Districts, and, in some particulars, with Lodges.

2. Masonic Courtesy. The Bodies, both Grand and Subordinate, of the four other Rites belong permanently to the American System; while a Grand Lodge or a Lodge cannot be in official relations with them there are many un-official relationships. The same is true of certain old and respected Side Orders, even though they are not Masonic.

3. Masonic Finance. This subject, including Masonic property, is almost wholly lacking in Mackey's treatise, but in late years has been bulking large in the enactments of Lodges and Grand Lodges, and is receiving an increasing amount of attention from Masonic Jurisconsults.

4. Matters relating to Petitioners and Candidates and to their preparation and education have become a large and independent subject; although Mackey's treatise discusses certain of the elements in it, his treatment is inadequate to the many-sidedness of that topic as it is now developed.

5. The whole subject of Side Orders, Clubs, Side Degrees, etc., is not touched upon by Mackey, but is receiving attention from every American Grand Lodge.

6. Masonic Districts, whether under a District Deputy Grand Master, or a District Grand Lecturer, or both, is referred to in passing by Mackey; but the District system

has grown to such proportions that a present-day writer on Jurisprudence would need to devote a chapter to it.

7. Both Masonic Parliamentary Law and Masonic Etiquette are separate and apart from Jurisprudence, nevertheless the three overlap, and an adequate work on Jurisprudence, brought up to date, must include a discussion of them.

These matters are more fully covered in subsequent chapters and in other Masonic books.

CHAPTER VI

MASONIC PARLIAMENTARY LAW

THE ancestors of English-speaking peoples were tribes and clans in Northern Europe and Britain who from the earliest beginnings had the custom of deciding matters which affected the whole population in "folk-moots," or popular assemblies, where each man had, directly or indirectly, a voice and a vote; and it is for this reason that many of the first written codes of law were little more than rules for conducting assemblies, for debate, and for balloting. In the English Common law, which is the basis of American civil law, these "rules of assembly," "principles of representation" and of "voice and of vote" bulk very large; and what is called "Parliamentary Law," the governing deliberative assemblies, belongs to its essence.

Parliamentary law, therefore, is law in its strict and original sense. If men meet in responsible assemblies, either as parties of the first part or as representatives of others, they are responsible, among themselves and to each other, not only for what they do but for the form in which they do it; and similarly they are responsible as a body to the community or to the State. If the action of a deliberative and responsible assembly comes into a civil court for review or adjudication that assembly's parliamentary law is germane to the question and may belong to the material evidence, because the law of the State may lie in the actions of such assemblies. From assemblies of one kind to assemblies of another kind details of procedure may differ widely, and usually they do, but in substance and principle they are everywhere the same.

A member of such an assembly has a stake in it and he may be materially affected by its actions; what it does may affect his good name, his reputation, or may concern him in his business, profession, calling, or work, or in his interests in property, or it may disturb him in the peace and contentment of his mind. For the same reason an assembly has a stake in each member; for he may injure its own reputation, may disrupt it, may disturb its peace and harmony, or may injure it in some of its material interests. The modes and forms of conducting business in responsible deliberative assemblies therefore come under the review, or the control, of the law of the State because property and reputation are involved, and where they are involved, there lies the law: and the fact that such an assembly may be private to the members, who are in a free association which governs itself and brooks no interference from without, does not mean that they can be a law unto themselves or can avoid the law of the State. If men as a group hold and use property, and receive, expend, appropriate, and have custody of monies, the civil laws appertaining to such matters, and their mode and manner of conducting such business must conform to the requirements of those laws.

This is the first of all facts for a Worshipful Master to grasp when he sits down to preside over a Lodge according to Masonic Parliamentary Law. The Masonic code differs in its forms from that of any other society, except such as are organized in imitation of the Fraternity, but it does not differ in substance or principle, and it is, like the code of other societies, at bottom nothing other than a means whereby the Lodge conforms in its modes and methods of conducting business to the requirements of the laws of the State. A Masonic Lodge, and as much so as a bank or a business concern, uses, owns, buys, or sells property, is responsible to its members and to the community, receives, banks, expends, and appropriates money, and its actions are material to the reputation and standing of its members, therefore when he is enforcing Parliamentary Law the Master is acting responsibly to the State as well as to his own superiors in the Fraternity, so that it behooves him, in a double sense, to make sure that he knows it.

Masonic Parliamentary Law is by these tokens sharply distinguished from the other bodies of observance which belong to established Masonic practice. Masonic Etiquette is a system, grounded in custom, to which belong the observances of courtesy and manners, as these appear under circumstances peculiar to Freemasonry, and are expected equally of all members and at all times. Masonic Deportment is that private behavior which Masonry expects of each and every member to the end that the business of a Lodge be not disturbed and that peace and harmony may prevail. Ritualism is a symbolic practice inherent in the conferring of the Degrees by which a man is made a Mason according to a due and regular form. Masonic Procedure is a set of rules by which it is ordained that a Lodge shall do certain things and in a certain order. The laws of the State do not control any of these bodies of observance, and even if that does not lighten a Master's responsibility to them (the Landmarks are also in them) it sets them in a class apart from Parliamentary Law, and it is an affront to reason and to reality to confuse the last named with any of the others.

The inwardness of Masonic Parliamentary Law reveals itself under analysis: (a) In essence, it is the civil law as it applies to deliberative assemblies and as that law holds under Masonic circumstances. (b) The general system of it comprises two particular forms; first, those practices which go according to legal forms required by civil law; second, those practices which are peculiar to Freemasonry, and go according to the requirements of the Landmarks. (c) The rule of procedure, which, in essence, goes according to the principle of precedence, according to which first things come first, second things come second, and so on forth. (d) The rules which govern debate, discussion, motions, and resolutions. (e) Written records, consisting of minutes, reports, resolutions, bills, receipts, etc., including their preservation in official archives. These principles of Masonic Parliamentary Law are among the fundamentals of the Regular Order of Business, to preserve and to conform to which is one of the Master's chief responsibilities.

Though Masonic Parliamentary Law conforms so perfectly to the requirements of the civil law that a Lodge need never come under the purview of the courts if it adheres to it faithfully, it is radically different in form and practice from parliamentary law as used in other similar societies—excepting those which are organized in imitation of Freemasonry. In ordinary societies such handbooks as Robert's *Rules of Order* and Cushing's *Manual* are the Bibles for every presiding officer, but those handbooks are useless to a Worshipful Master because Freemasonry has so many practices peculiar to itself. Perhaps the most radical difference between a Lodge and any other body lies in the office of the Master; in other bodies the Chairman or President or Moderator does little more than preside; the Worshipful Master has executive duties of another kind; he makes decisions of large importance on

PRESIDING OFFICERS

Most bodies *choose their own*. Only *Master or Wardens* can preside and open Lodge. When all three absent, Lodge cannot be opened *without dispensation* from Grand Master.

APPEALS

May usually be taken from decisions of chairman to membership. *No appeal* from *Master's rulings* except to *Grand Master*.

MOTIONS

The *will* of any body must be *embodied in a motion*. Debate permissible. Though he should not do so without cause, *Master may forbid discussion*. No appeal. Decision is by vote. Motions are:
1. Principal or Main.
2. Subsidiary.
3. Incidental.
4. Privileged.

MOTIONS—HOW MADE—PROCEDURE

Maker rises. Addresses Master. When recognized, makes motion. *Master may refuse* to entertain motion. No appeal. *Unless seconded, motion fails*. Written out if Master or any Brother requests. *Master* may *stop debate at any time*. No appeal. During discussion a *peremptory* motion for *"the previous question"* (to stifle debate) though allowed by "Rules of Order" is *never permissible in Lodges*. After *reasonable* amount of discussion Master may permit *motion to adjourn debate*. Should be made only by one who has not *already spoken*. While *pending*, all *debate suspended*. If defeated, *not renewable* until other business intervenes. *Debate* is *resumed where it left off.* Unless By-Laws permit, all may speak but once. *Master* only may *allow second speeches.* Usually, by consent, permitted in public meetings. *Maker* of motion may *speak again*—closing debate but only by way of *reply* or *rebuttal.* If new matter presented or, if amended, *all may speak again.*

VOTE—HOW TAKEN

By Ayes or Noes—or show of hands. There is *no* so-called *"Sign of the Order."* If a sign is in general use, proper reference is the *"usual voting sign of the order."* If Master (or any Brother) is *doubtful,* another vote may be taken. Master decides result. No appeal. *In case of tie, Master* has second and *deciding vote.* After vote taken Master announces result. If division is demanded, it should always be allowed. Division is decided by *rising vote. All must vote unless excused.* When counted Master announces result. No appeal.

SUBSIDIARY MOTIONS

In order of precedence under general Rules of Order are:

1. To adjourn.
2. To lay on table.
3. For the Previous Question.
4. To postpone to a time certain.
5. To send to Committee.
6. To amend.
7. To postpone indefinitely.

MASONIC LODGES:

1. and 3. of the above are never permitted, so the *Fixed Order of Precedence* (as laid down by Mackey) is:

1. To lay on table.

2. To postpone indefinitely.
3. To postpone to a time certain.
4. To send to Committee.
5. To amend.

Though it is last in priority, we consider (5)—To amend—first, as it is most important and in most general use.

TO AMEND AND AMENDMENTS TO AMENDMENTS (only one allowed)

Same rules in Lodges as in general Rules of Order.

Motions: (1) *To lay on table* (2) *To postpone Indefinitely* are the same as those used in most public bodies. (3) In Lodges motions to *postpone* to a *time certain* differ only from general procedure in that the time set must be during *that session* whereas in other bodies it may be at *that* or a *later session*. May be amended. Debate is only on expediency of postponement. (4) *To send to committee.* *Automatic* if it goes to Standing Committee of Lodge. If to Special Committee, referred by Master or by Motion. May be Amended. Reconsidered.

INCIDENTAL QUESTIONS

(1) Order. (2) Reading of Papers. (3) Withdrawing motion or Papers. (4) Suspending By-Laws. (5) Voting by recorded Ayes or Noes. In General bodies, are always in order. Have priority. Subject to Subsidiary Motions. (1) *Questions of Order* concern *present* action of body. They are (a) Kind of Motion. (b) When to be made. (c) Priority. (d) Limits of Debate. (e) Restrictions on Speakers. *Only one main motion* before Lodge *at a time*. *Speakers* must *address Master only,* who designates who has floor by pronouncing his name. May be interrupted only by Master or for Point of Order. No personalities. Master may order persistent offender ejected from Lodge. All must speak

only *to the question*. Master sole judge as to that. No appeal. *Speak only when motion before Lodge*. If Master does not raise Question of Order, any Brother may. Addresses Master (without waiting to be recognized) and says, "I rise to a Point of Order." Master says, "State your Point of Order." When stated, Master says, "Your Point is (or is not) well taken." Speaker either *resumes* or *is cautioned or stopped*. No appeal. (2) Pertinent Papers must be read if Master or any Brother requests. (3) *Withdrawal of motions or papers*. If no objection, *consent assumed*. Unanimous to withdraw motions. Majority to withdraw papers. Any time before vote taken. If amendment proposed, cannot withdraw motion unless amendment previously withdrawn or defeated. Can *never withdraw petition for degrees*. (4) *Suspending By-Laws*. Most bodies can do so if By-Laws permit or by unanimous vote. *By-Laws cannot be* changed or *suspended* by Lodges as *Grand Lodges must approve* all By-Laws and all changes before they become effective. (5) *Aye and No vote* (to put members on record) *not permitted in Lodges*. Allowed in other bodies. Members may change vote before it is announced. Vote may be reconsidered.

QUESTIONS OF PRIVILEGE

Concern *rights of Lodge* and *individual members*. Have priority. They are: (1) Reputation of Lodge. (2) Character of members. (3) Secrecy or safety of Lodge. Always in order. Brother rises, addresses Master (without waiting to be recognized) and says, "I rise to a Question of Privilege." Master says, "State your Question." When stated, Master rules. No appeal. *If negative, business is resumed. If affirmative, Master may decide it then or later*. Always in order. Subject to Subsidiary Motions. Their *priority* also *attaches to any report* on them.

PRIVILEGED QUESTIONS

1. Privilege of (a) Lodge (b) its Members.
2. Adjournment.
3. Reconsideration.
4. Special settings.

(1) Already covered. (2) Never applies in Lodges. (3) In most bodies may be made that day or session, or next day or session. In Lodges only same day or session. (a) After Lodge is closed legislation can be changed only by rescinding or repealing. (b) Only those voting with *prevailing side* may move or second motion to *reconsider*. (3a) Affects only matters still *remaining under Lodge control.*

1. Not debatable if original motion was not.
2. Takes majority vote only (though original motion may have required larger vote).
3. If moved in time (and then withdrawn) it cannot be renewed if Lodge has closed.
4. No other motion can be made to reconsider, if one is pending or has been defeated.
5. Subject to Subsidiary Motions.
6. While pending, all operation of original motion is entirely suspended.
7. If carried, original motion reverts to its status *just before passage.* Also
8. If carried, original motion is *up for immediate action* subject to Subsidiary Motions.

NO RECONSIDERATION OF BALLOT ON CANDIDATE

Permitted in many bodies. *Never allowed in Masonic Lodges.* Ballot being secret, *no one is qualified* to make or second a Motion *to Reconsider.* Only Master may order another ballot and then usually only when single black-ball appears. Second Ballot must be at same meeting. All those who voted before must be present to vote again. (This matter is usually covered by Grand Lodge rules or Lodge By-Laws.) Neither the Grand Master nor the Grand Lodge can authorize, or order, subsequent ballots.

SPECIAL SETTINGS—PRIVILEGED

Have priority. In Lodges only later hour in same session may be set. At time fixed, *have first precedence*. If Master (or some member) does not call them up, they lose priority. They take precedence in the order in which they were made.

SUGGESTED ORDER OF LODGE BUSINESS

(1) Open Lodge. (2) Read Minutes and approve (at stated meetings only). (3) Receiving Petitions. (4) Reports on Petitions. (5) Ballot on Candidates. (6) Reports of Special Committees. (7) Reports of Standing Committees. (8) Unfinished Business. (9) New Business. (10) Initiation. (11) Reading of rough draft of minutes for information and verification. (12) Close Lodge.

COMMITTEES

STANDING—Concerned with *general* Masonic business such as Finance, Investigating, Lodge Room, Charity, etc. Appointed for entire Masonic year, at start of year. Grand Lodge rules or Lodge By-Laws usually provide for them. *Master appoints all committees unless otherwise stated.* In that case Lodge may elect, or select members by motion.

SPECIAL COMMITTEES

As to appointment, same rules apply as for Standing Committees. If by motion, maker is usually put on the

Committee. First named is Chairman. He calls first meeting of Committee at suitable time and place and after due notice. Committees may select own Chairman. Seldom done because discourteous. Preferably as few members as possible. Odd number best. Then always a majority. Appoint only those generally favorable to committee purpose. Members should attend all meetings. Majority is quorum and may act for all. Must meet and not merely canvass members' opinions. Informal. May consider only matters referred to them. Chairman, or other member designated, prepares report.

COMMITTEE REPORT

May be (1) Opinion only. (2) Opinion and proposed legislation. (3) Legislation only. Should be signed by all who agree. Must be signed by majority. The Master or Lodge may refuse to receive report. That discharges committee and kills its objective. If no objection, when presented, report is received and read by maker or Secretary. A motion to receive is then out of order as already received when read. If final report, Special Committee is *automatically discharged*. Reports of Standing Committees are always in order. If report is (1) Opinion only—a motion to adopt it accomplishes nothing. If (2) or (3) a motion to adopt also passes the proposed legislation. A motion to recommit revives the Committee which resumes consideration. May recommit with instructions to prepare legislation. Cannot recommit and instruct committee to change its opinion. Instead should reject report and pass legislation to suit majority. May adopt motion declaring opposition to Committee's report. Committee may request more time. If it neglects, or refuses, to report, matter may be taken from Committee. The majority report for the entire Committee—no minority report. When one is attempted it is only opinion of individuals and cannot be adopted. Merely a proposed amendment, or substitute, for majority report.

INVESTIGATING COMMITTEE

Automatically receives petitions for membership (as provided by Grand Lodge Rules or Lodge By-Laws). No subsidiary Motions apply. Must lay over one month or until next stated meeting. Full inquiry should be made as to both character and capacity. No subsidiary Motions apply to report when made. Ballot at once without discussion. If report unfavorable, no ballot necessary as at least two Brethren opposed. Some authorities hold ballot must be taken anyway.

FILLING BLANKS

If blanks in Motion, Master puts first *largest amount* or *longest* time proposed. Continues vote on proposals until majority agree.

DIVISION OF QUESTION

Master should divide any question if he deems it advisable or should allow division, if demanded, and if question is divisible and if each part can stand alone. Master decides. No appeal. May be done any time before vote taken.

AMENDMENTS TO BY-LAWS

Must be made *exactly* as By-Laws provide. Any change in a proposed amendment must be made *at the same session* if it is to be passed at same time as original proposed amendment. If it must lay over no change in substance or wording is later permitted from its form when introduced unless it again lays over the required time.

NOMINATION TO OFFICE

Permitted in most bodies. Formerly allowed in Masonic elections but now all elect without nomination. Correct form is "Select some *suitable* Brother to serve you as (name of office)."

APPROVING MINUTES

Read and approved only at stated meetings. May be read at Special Meetings *only for information.* May be corrected, but never altered, for the purpose of changing previous Lodge action. *If a correct record, minutes must be approved.*

CHAPTER VII

MASONIC ETIQUETTE

ETIQUETTE is a mode of behavior which goes according to fixed rules. The name itself makes that clear, being a shortened form of the French *a la carte,* "according to the card." It carries the picture of a set of rules written down, a copy distributed to each man or woman involved, and with the implied proviso that unless a man carries out the rules he will be excluded from the occasion or the assembly. An act of etiquette is thus by definition one that cannot be left to the individual to see or to carry out according to his own taste; he conforms to it whether he himself sees any good reason for doing so or not.

Any organization such as Freemasonry makes these rules because it needs them. It needs them in order to carry out its own purposes. Since the rules are thus good for the organization as a whole that good affects each member in it; it is because of this that a given rule of etiquette is not an empty or meaningless formality, arbitrarily enacted and tyrannically imposed, like an act of mummery performed for the mere sake of performing it. An act of Masonic Etiquette is thus some movement, action, gesture, or speech performed at a given time and place, in a certain manner, and according to rule fixed and imposed by the Fraternity itself.

Though in appearance Etiquette may often be confused

with Decorum the two are, in principle, wholly unlike each other. Masonic Decorum means that each Mason as he is among his Brethren so comports himself as not to call attention to himself or to create disturbance in his neighborhood. Only the individual himself can ever know whether a given action will create disturbance or not, because it depends on the circumstances; under some circumstances he may speak aloud to the Brother next to him without occasioning disturbance, under others the same words would disturb the whole Lodge. It is expected of him that he will know for himself when to speak or to keep silence, when to move about or when to remain seated; and so on forth. Decorum goes according to one fixed principle binding on each one alike: that the peace and harmony of the Lodge shall not be disturbed by gaucheries and blunders of private nature.

There are matters of character which do not lie in the control of any man to alter, emend, amend, or to suspend them; are independent of personality, circumstances, or conditions, but are laws among the other laws of God, and are binding on the whole of mankind. There are qualities which belong to men as men, and are carried with them wherever they go; among these are such qualities and graces as politeness, courtesy, manners, tact, taste, consideration of others. Freemasonry requires of each of its members that he have character and possess these qualities but it makes sure of them *before* a man is admitted to membership; a petitioner for the Degrees must be worthy and well-qualified, be under the tongue of good report, and come well recommended.

Masonic Etiquette thus stands sharply distinguished from among those other requirements which it may superficially resemble; it consists of a set of rules adopted or enacted by the Craft for its own purposes, each rule com-

ing into operation at a given time and place or under a
certain set of circumstances, requiring that something be
said or done according to a formal pattern. Since each rule
is enacted because Freemasonry has need of it, it has a
purpose; since that purpose is a rational one, there is a
reasonable explanation for it, and therefore Masonic
Etiquette can be *understood* as well as practiced. Thus,
for one example, if the Senior Deacon at one instant in a
Ceremony bows toward the East it has a purpose—perhaps
to signal the fact that the Worshipful Master is about to
approach, or to bring an episode in the Ritual to a close,
etc.; or, for another example, if a Grand Master is received
in full form it is to indicate officially that the Lodge has
now passed from one presiding Officer to another.

Certain details of Masonic Etiquette may differ from
one Lodge to another, or from one Grand Jurisdiction to
another; in some cases one Lodge or Grand Lodge will
have a rule; another will not; in other cases two Lodges
or Grand Lodges will have the same rule but may carry
it out in a different form; it is because any Masonic Body
works under circumstances or conditions peculiar to itself
and over which it has no control. The whole body of
Masons themselves work in a changing world. If Etiquette
differs it does so only in the same manner, to the same
extent, and owing to the same circumstances, that Lodges
and Grand Lodges differ.

But while such differences are inevitable and do not
disturb the principles of Masonic Etiquette they make it
impossible for any book to lay down detailed instructions
for the carrying out of many of the fixed rules. Those
instructions are available elsewhere. The one and only
purpose of this book is to describe Etiquette in its principle and outline and thereby to assist to a better *understanding* of it.

It is on this basis that the following sections on each of a large number of our rules of Etiquette are included in this book. Certain of them are rules fixed and unchangeable everywhere and always, in Freemasonry and for that reason have the character of Landmarks; certain others are in outline and purpose everywhere the same but vary in their minutiae; others of the rules may be in force in some Lodges or Grand Lodges, not in others at all. In any of these cases the descriptions and explanations given here, however detailed, are for the purpose of making clear the point or purpose of each rule discussed; a reader must make sure for himself what form is used in his own Lodge or Grand Jurisdiction.

A Lodge member usually learns Etiquette as he goes along, from receiving the Degrees, from sitting in Lodge, from the Opening and Closing ceremonies; but if he does not attend regularly, or if he is confronted by an unfamiliar situation, he will turn to some officer for guidance, and usually to the Worshipful Master. The Master is exemplar, judge, and teacher in Etiquette. He must have a grasp of it beyond that of a member or of any other officer; it is because this is true that most of the sections below are framed with him in mind.

He can assist himself to a general knowledge of Etiquette, which is so laborious to learn, detail by detail, if he studies it as divided into a number of large classifications, each one with a heading of its own. These headings will be seen to be self-explanatory:

1. The Etiquette of the Individual. Outside the Lodge or any other Masonic assembly, each member has Masonic duties of his own which he carries on in the name of Masonry; he may visit a sick Brother, write a Masonic letter, engage in Masonic discussion, etc. They are his own acts, nevertheless in certain kinds of them it is needed

that each and every Mason shall do them in the same way, and in a number of these that "same way" is provided for by a rule of Etiquette. Thus a private Mason in private Masonic correspondence will address Lodge or Grand Lodge officers correctly by their titles, etc.

2. The Etiquette of the Lodge. The rules coming under this head hold of the Lodge when it is in session in its own Room or whenever it acts as a Lodge outside its room; the Lodge as a body, therefore, is the point or purpose of each one of them, and they can be explained in the terms of that purpose.

3. The Etiquette of Grand Lodge. Certain rules in the Grand Lodge are identical with those of a Lodge yet are not repetitious of Lodge rules, carried over into another place, but are as much the Grand Lodge's own rules as if they belonged to it exclusively; other of its rules are wholly its own, and are for needs not found elsewhere.

4. The Etiquette of Masonic Comity. Comity consists of fraternal activities and relations as between one Lodge and another, between a Lodge and its District or its Grand Lodge, between a Grand Lodge and other Grand Lodges, between a Lodge or a Grand Lodge and a Body in some other Masonic Rite. Each rule in comity has a Masonic Body as its point; and to maintain harmonious relations between it and other Bodies is its purpose.

5. The Etiquette of the Fraternity as a whole. The rules belonging under this head hold as between Freemasonry and the outside world. Because they belong to Freemasonry as a whole they are the same everywhere in the Craft, in principle if not in form. Under the Ancient Landmarks Masonry can act toward non-Masons, bodies of non-Masons, Communities, States, and Nations but only insofar as those acts fall within the limits of "Masonic purposes."

The details of Masonic Etiquette differ from one Grand Jurisdiction to another. For that reason you may find in the following sections certain usages not practiced in your own Grand Jurisdiction, and fail to find certain other usages which are. This is unavoidable. But since the discussion in each section concerns only substance and principle, conflicts with local usages have been avoided to the utmost possible extent.

GOOD MANNERS

The charm of good manners! Like love, or beauty, or music, it conquers where it stands, without force or argument, by its own inherent shining, and is its own justification and reward. If we study etiquette, which is its code and principle, it is because we have been already won to its claims and desire to shape ourselves to its appeal, whether it be in the uses of politeness, gracious behavior, pleasing conduct, deportment, courtliness or any other of those amenities of word and act by which among his fellows a man is distinguished as a gentleman.

Masonry, like every separate circle in human society, has an etiquette of its own. Its foundations were laid by those Operative Masons to whom, being cathedral builders, architecture was more an art than a trade, and who learned refinement from their daily work. Its superstructure arose, generation by generation, through the decay of cathedral building, the two centuries of transition, through the formative period of the Speculative Craft, and has been completed, to the stage we have it by two centuries of experience in tens of thousands of Ancient Craft teaching the art of gentle manners more by practice than Lodges, each of which, since it binds a man in many contacts to his fellows, has been itself a school of deportment, by precept.

In principle Masonic etiquette belongs to the empire of good manners, that code by which gentlemen the world over govern their conduct; but this principle with us is found to apply in two directions: on the one hand it becomes a manifestation of respect for the Craft as a whole; on the other hand it is a form of courtesy to the individual.

Freemasonry solicits no man to join it; permits no man to make innovations in its body of principles and Landmarks; its candidates come of their own free will and because they have heard good reports of its reputation and formed a favorable opinion of its work. And by all means, throughout its entire system, and through all its bodies and degrees, by tradition, Landmark, usage, custom, law, rule, edict, regulation, and constitution, it is in every way secured that a Mason shall stand to it in an attitude of reverence and respect. Of that reverence and respect etiquette is one of the forms.

From among the many who feel a desire for the honor of membership in its assemblies it selects the few who are shown to have the necessary qualifications; and once these are admitted they are by that fact marked each and every one with the seal of equal fellowship, and placed in a relation of the same rights, privileges, and duties with all others, no distinctions of wealth, station, rank, race, or creed being then permitted. Among these members it is a principal effort of the Craft to maintain unity and harmony, and it is one of the sovereign duties laid on every one of its officials to be responsible for avoiding or prohibiting acts or conduct on the part of any that might militate against the Craft's being "a centre of union, and the means of conciliating true friendships among persons that must otherwise have remained at a perpetual distance." When this spirit and intent of the Fraternity brings itself to focus upon the individual it takes the form of a sincere courtesy, and it is to give expression to this courtesy that much of Masonic etiquette exists.

There is a certain grave beauty in the practice of that etiquette. The Masonic life, as it is lived out in our assemblies is a conscious work of art, with each and every part co-ordinated to every other, and instinct with the feeling of the whole; if a man enters into that system without preparation or forethought, and trusting only his instincts, his manner will strike an awkward note, like a discord jangling across a strain of music; but if he has trained himself in his part and caught the spirit of the whole, the genius of Freemasonry will shine through his actions, will express itself through him, just as, under other conditions, it expresses itself through ritual, symbol, law, philosophy, fellowship and daily deed. To have one's self thus become a part of a great and living whole is a kind of satisfying pleasure nothing else can give, a participation in the very life of beauty, appreciated as much by the beholder as by the actor. This ability to confer pleasure upon one's fellows when gathered in communication or in ceremony is not the least of etiquette's rewards.

Harmony is the first law of the Lodge as it is of heaven. Where discord enters, Freemasonry leaves. For one man to live in unity with another belongs to the very essence of our Royal Art; if unity is destroyed fellowship becomes a pile of ashes, and the sun, moon and stars of brotherhood are eclipsed by fog or storm. Since it is the nature of decorum to nurture and protect harmony, etiquette is a bulwark of the Craft, a certain insurance against many of those schisms and discords by which so much of the good work of a Lodge may be destroyed in so short a time. "You talk about forms," exclaimed Goethe to a disciple, "as if substance could be formless; neglect form and see how long you will have any substance!"

Our etiquette also is a guarantee of equality in the Craft's treatment of its members. Imagine it to be destroyed by a stroke over night, and Masons left to act out of prejudices or whims! The poor man would be snubbed by the rich, the timid overwhelmed by the brazen, the elected official would lord it over the layman, favoritism, class-consciousness, vanity, snobbery, and all the forms of an ugly secular worldliness would cut this way and that across each Lodge until Freemasonry would at last succumb to those very passions it now exists to control. Equality would be gone, that equality in which each man is treated with the same courtesy as every other; the sword would replace the Level among the Working Tools.

UTILITARIAN VALUE

At the same time, and by the same token, Masonic etiquette possesses a utility, the full extent of which has often escaped notice; that utility consists in the power to enable many men of different abilities, and without rehearsal, to act in concert through elaborate ceremonies or complex activities—a power etiquette shares with ritual. Consider some such ceremony as the conferring of a Degree, the installation of officers, the reception of a Grand Lodge officer, a funeral ceremony, a public procession; the part each is to play is to a large extent prescribed in the Standard Work, or in some other form of words or acts committed to memory; but over and above this are a hundred and one required observances belonging to etiquette which are necessary to the harmonious exemplification of the whole. These observances exist already, each of a careful design that fits it exactly for its function. By means of these pre-existent forms, learned by the participants, a large number of men, unrehearsed, are enabled to work smoothly in unison. This requirement, were there no other, would make etiquette a necessity in such a society as ours.

In speaking of Masonic etiquette it is necessary to emphasize the word "Masonic." Our etiquette is a unique creation, peculiar to the Fraternity, "flesh of its flesh and bone of its bone," absurd, as all misfits are absurd, if used outside of its own setting, but complete and beautiful within the Craft's own framework; some parts of it are optional, left to the good taste of the individual; other parts are prescribed by usage or by law, written or unwritten; the whole of it belongs integrally to the organic body of Freemasonry and as such stands on a level with the Landmarks, the Constitutions, the Ritual, and the Symbols.

MASONIC ETIQUETTE

Aged and Infirm
Altar
Anteroom
Apron
Ballot
Bible Presentation
Church Etiquette
Church Service
Decorum
Discussion In Lodge
Discussion of Masonry
Directions to Lodge Room
District Deputy Grand Masters
Distinguished Visitors
Dress
Emergencies
Entrance During Meetings
Etiquette Regarding Officers
Examination of Visitors
Flag of Nation
Gifts to Candidates
Gloves
Great Lights
Hat (The Master's)
Information on Etiquette
Inquisitives
Insignia Uses and Abuses
Ladies at Lodge Affairs
Landmarks and Etiquette
Letters to Grand Officers
Memorial Services in Lodge
Non-Masons at Masonic Meetings
Objections From The Floor

MASONIC ETIQUETTE—continued

AGED AND INFIRM

If a member is infirm he may be assisted to enter the Lodge and to salute, on the arm of the Junior Deacon; and if he requires it, a chair or special seat may be provided for him. However, it is not fitting in etiquette to attract attention to his infirmity by paying him special heed, remarking on his presence, etc. If an aged member cannot attend Lodge some mention of him should be occasionally made at a Communication and the Master should see that he is visited and otherwise reminded that he is present in the minds of his Brethren. A visitor should come to him as an emissary from the Lodge, speaking officially in its behalf, not as a private friend only, and for that reason should act as he would act in Lodge, and in Masonic decorum.

ALTAR

The altar is a perfect cube in shape. In Lodges throughout America it stands at the center of the Lodge room. It is the place of prayer; a pedestal on which rests the Three Great Lights; the Lesser Lights stand beside it; the obligation is taken in its presence; the Worshipful Master greets the Candidate across it; and it is, in addition, a symbol and emblem of religion. The ground between it and the East is a sacred precinct which is not transgressed by officers or members during Lodge communications. Members or visitors stand before it to salute the East when entering or leaving the room. It therefore belongs to etiquette for any Masons when near it to stand with dignity and to act with reverence; and it should not be draped or covered with flags, bunting, or draperies of any kind or have on it any banners, devices, embroideries, etc., which carry the name or insignia of any individual, or association, or organization other than that of the Lodge or the Grand Lodge. It should be kept clean, its paint or varnish not marred or cracked or scratched, and the top and foot-rest, if upholstered, should never be shabby.

ANTE-ROOM

The ante-room is a part of the Lodge room, stands in its own precincts, is not a separate room like a club or a lobby, and therefore the decorum and etiquette of the Lodge room governs it. Since the Tiler is in charge of it, in the same sense that the Master is in charge of the Lodge room, he is responsible to the Master to see that etiquette is observed. It should be clean and neat, with no litter lying about, the furniture in place, aprons correctly placed and piled, the light where it belongs, and nothing stored in it which does not belong in it. Loud talking, joking, noise, needless moving about, these are not permissible. The Tiler should introduce himself to a visiting Brother the moment he enters the Ante-Room; and should see that he has a seat, if he must wait before entering the Lodge room or while waiting for an Examining Committee. The door to the Lodge room is in the Junior Warden's custody, not the Tiler's; the Tiler should never open it or talk through it until after knocking. When a member of the Lodge enters the Ante-Room after Lodge is opened he is in it to observe a Ceremony of Entrance, and this Ceremony should be conducted by the Tiler according to a fixed procedure, and the procedure should be invariable, never altered for any member or officer.

APRON

Symbolically, and in principle, the Apron should be white because it is an emblem of innocence; but it also is the badge of Masons, not only in the eyes of the public but also among themselves; and since there are grades and ranks in the Lodge, along with grades and ranks in Councils, Chapters, Commanderies and Consistories, the badge must not only show that a man is a Mason but, in many instances, must show the body to which he belongs and his grade or rank in it. It is not within the province of Etiquette to decide any of these details of color, size, shape, or ornamentation.

Etiquette requires that a Mason shall remember that the Apron is not a piece of cloth but an insignium; as an insignium it denotes membership and rank, and it is therefore membership and rank that a man is concerned with when he is handling or wearing it. He will not expect to find it lying in a miscellaneous heap on a chair in a corner, will not toss it carelessly aside when the Lodge is closed, will not snatch it up as if it were a rag, and when he ties it on and wears it about, will do so with a feeling of what it signifies; and will wear it only at the times and places called for by good form, not when going about outside the Ante-room on errands or when at chores.

BALLOT

The Ballot is both secret and inviolable. When it is taken the act is fateful for the Candidate and momentous for the Lodge and it is an official act by each member in turn and by the Lodge as a whole, therefore it has a legal sanction and must be conducted according to solemn rules. It is Etiquette for the Lodge room to be in complete silence, without whispering or conversing or moving about, or discussion of the Candidate, or any information about how a member has voted; the officers should remain at their stations and places in silence and dignity, and such of them as participate in spreading, inspecting, and declaring it, should act in strict decorum. This period of Etiquette and Decorum includes the declaring of it by the Master, the removal of the Ballot Box, and the return of the participating officers to their places.

BIBLE PRESENTATION

Where the presentation of a Bible to the Candidate is made regularly and by action of the Lodge, it has an official status and stands on the same level as the established Monitorial Work. A place in the ceremonies is preserved for it. The presentation is made in due form. Usually the presentation follows a now generally established pattern: (1) At the end of the Degree, and before the Candidate is seated on the side-lines, the Senior Deacon presents him at the Altar. (2) While he is standing, and with the Senior Deacon at his side, the Master, Chaplain or other Officer, or a member he may have appointed, presents the Bible, and when doing so addresses the Candidate for some two or three minutes on the Bible and its place in Masonry, using either a prepared speech or else extemporizing on the spot. (3) After that is concluded the Master bows, the Candidate and Senior Deacon bow (the Candidate does not speak), and after the Master is seated in the East the Senior Deacon leads the Candidate to a seat.

CHURCH ETIQUETTE

If Masons attend a church separately, each one going by himself and finding his own seat, even though the service has been arranged for them, no Masonic Etiquette is involved. If Masons first meet together at the Lodge room and go from there in a body, they are under the rules of their own Etiquette until they arrive at the church door, and will be again after they have left the door at the end of the service; but when they reach the door at the beginning they come under the Church's own etiquette, as it will be exemplified by the Pastor and his assistants, and continue to be under it until their departure.

CHURCH SERVICE

If a pastor who is himself a Mason is to preach a sermon to a body of Masons in his own church, he does not meet with his Brethren at the Lodge room but goes to the church, and there remains near the entrance until they arrive; greets the Worshipful Master; has them conducted as a body to the pews reserved for them. He can announce at the beginning of his sermon that the members of a Lodge are in attendance as a body, and, if he wishes, may address himself to them, but it will be a sermon that he delivers, not a lecture on Masonry; for the Masons are there to attend a religious service and not to hear an address about themselves. If the pastor is not a Mason he greets the Masons as a body when they arrive, and has them seated; he can then recognize their presence during his opening services and extend them a welcome as fellow worshipers, but it is scarcely in order for him to deliver a Masonic sermon; he conducts his regular service of worship, and the Masons are there among the other worshipers.

DECORUM

It is impossible to draw a hard and fast line between Etiquette and Decorum; there is however a sharp contrast between the principles of the two: in Etiquette a Mason is controlled by rules of manner and behavior at certain times and places in which he has no voice, because they are governed by Masonic law and usage; so that it is for him to learn them and to carry them out; the principle of Decorum stands at the opposite pole, for it includes manner and behavior in the Lodge room as it is in the Mason himself to decide and control; the essence of it lies in a Mason, when present in Lodge, not attracting attention to himself and not creating disturbance. Thus, it is Etiquette to salute at the Altar, and while that is an act of good manners it is one required by the rules of the Lodge; it is Decorum not to talk out loud during the conferring of a Degree, and that is good manners as required by a man's own sense of dignity. If he talks aloud, disturbing the Lodge, *he* does it, and it is therefore for him not to. He must decide his own Decorum in the same way that the Lodge decides his Etiquette. There is one point at which the two converge; it is when the Master must act to restore decorum; there is an Etiquette in his so doing, of which the principle is that he shall rebuke disturbances in such a manner as not to be of itself a disturbing action; quietly, promptly, without personal feeling, and attracting as little attention as possible; a glance of the eye oftentimes is sufficient for the purpose, or a soft tap of the gavel.

DISCUSSION IN LODGE

Lodge room discussion consists of a member's addressing himself to a subject or a question after it has arisen; its

Etiquette consists of the manner in which it is done. A member is free to speak only when it is in order; he must rise; must salute and address himself to the East; must not begin to speak until recognized; must speak to the point; and must permit no acrimoniousness, personalities, or ill feeling in what he says or in his tone, feeling, or manner of saying it; must then salute, and sit down. It is a rule of Masonry that controversial questions are never in order, nor discussions of such non-Masonic subjects as politics and religion, but these matters are outside of Etiquette. The Master, however, has an Etiquette of his own in dealing with them; he either requests the speaker to avoid forbidden subjects and permits the speaker to continue; or, if the speaker ignores his request, the Master then rules the speaker out of order, upon which the speaker immediately is seated.

DISCUSSION OF MASONRY

If a Mason is at a table, or in a circle of conversation, or in some group where a discussion has arisen and the subject of Masonry enters the discussion, private Masonic Etiquette provides that he may keep silent if he desires. If the discussion is acrimonious, controversial, and may be aimed at Masonry he is expected to remain silent. If, however, he can give information about the Fraternity, and on such facts as are permissible to be known to the public, there is no reason for him not to do so.

DIRECTIONS TO LODGE ROOM

If a Lodge has its rooms in a building not its own, on the second or third floor, perhaps, to be reached by elevators, stairs, hallways, or is in a Masonic Temple among many other rooms, it may be difficult for a visitor to find his way to it from the street entrance. In that case the

Lodge ought to have a placard or sign near the street entrance, and the directions on it should be complete—often it is of small assistance to give nothing but a room number.

DISTRICT DEPUTY GRAND MASTER

In Grand Jurisdictions which employ the District Deputy Grand Master system, a District Deputy on an official visit is received with an etiquette which reflects the fact that he is the personal representative of the Grand Master, and when he is in the Lodge room it is as if the Grand Master were present in person. After he enters the Ante-room he announces that he is about to enter (a Master could not exclude a District Deputy); he is received at the Altar by the Worshipful Master and by him is conducted to the East, where he receives the gavel. After he enters on an official visit (he is not required to announce it in advance) he is never permitted to seat himself on the sidelines, unless it is at his own request. A Master cannot fail in his Etiquette if at all times he receives a District Deputy with the deference owed to the Grand Master.

DISTINGUISHED VISITORS

If a visiting Brother unexpectedly arrives who, because of his title or standing in the Craft, or for some similar reason, is one that the Master will wish to present to the Lodge, he may follow any of three general procedures: (1) Meet him at the Altar and there introduce him, after which he instructs the Senior Deacon to conduct the visitor to a seat. (2) Stand to salute and remain standing until the Senior Deacon has conducted the visitor to the East upon instruction by the Master, introduce the visitor from the East, give him a seat there. (3) At the time of the reception, or at any suitable or convenient time, ask the visitor to address the Lodge.

DRESS

A member dresses as the occasion requires. He will not wear clothes which will attract attention or create disturbance. It is when in the anteroom that he must adjust his clothing; put on his Apron, his insignia, his jewels. In some Masonic assemblies dress may be informal, as when it is too hot for coats; at others formal, or at least careful, dress is in order and a Master may wish to signify as much in his notice or announcement. In some Lodges the officers are required to be in formal dress; in others they are expected to be in formal dress at some occasions, in mufti at others; it is for the Master or the Lodge to decide. But it is in keeping with the spirit of the Fraternity for each and every Lodge to require of them formal dress on certain occasions because the occasions themselves are formal —as at the installation of officers, receptions of a Grand Master, etc. The principal point for etiquette in Masonic dress is one concerning members who hold rank; they should have their regalia, insignia, and jewels in correct form, properly placed, and in good condition.

EMERGENCIES

If an emergency arises from outside the room which must be brought to the attention of the Lodge the Senior Warden is first apprised; he then takes action at his own discretion, may rise and address the Master, etc. If the emergency is one that affects only a member, the Senior Warden is apprised first, and he may then deal with it or call out the member, etc., without addressing the Master or interfering with the proceedings of the Lodge. If a member present in Lodge is confronted by an emergency, slips and falls, is taken ill, etc., the Senior Warden acts immediately and at his own discretion.

ENTRANCE DURING MEETINGS

No member of the Lodge or visiting Brother enters from the Preparation Room. When entering from the Anteroom after Lodge is open he waits until signaled by the Tiler, steps through the door and advances in due form to the Altar, salutes, the Worshipful Master returning the salute, either sitting or standing. If the Master is engaged, the entering Brother stands before the Senior Warden, who rises; makes a salute, and receives a salute. He then finds his way to the nearest seat. In either form of entering, it is a ceremonious action on the side of both the Lodges and the Brother, and Etiquette requires that it be correctly performed. If a Brother ignores the Etiquette, or is unfamiliar with it, the Senior Warden may whisper instructions in his ear for him to follow.

ETIQUETTE REGARDING OFFICERS

An office has a station or place of its own in the Lodge room, with duties, dignities, and perogatives inherent in it. A form of Etiquette, accorded to one officer, represents those properties of his office, and therefore is not directed to him personally. A slovenly manner of saluting, of approaching the East or any other station, of standing, and of speaking to an officer, is a reflection on the Lodge for a failure to give to the offices that respect which belongs to them. If a Master himself exacts of every member, and of every other officer, a faithful rendering of the form of Etiquette that is to be accorded to his own office, it will create a more faithful observance of the form at each and every other station or place.

EXAMINATION OF VISITORS

The substance of an examination is fixed by law, and is not in the province of Etiquette, but the manner of it is.

The Examining Committee withdraws with the visitor to a private place; they are in an official relationship to him and therefore their manners are formal; and they should have it in mind that their only purpose is to satisfy themselves that the examinee is, or is not, a Regular Master Mason in good standing—they are not called upon to test his proficiency in the Ritual or to be personally inquisitive. Once the examination has satisfied them they conduct the visitor to the Ante-room and introduce him to the Tiler, who in turn hands him over to the Junior Deacon for escort to the Altar.

If the examining committee has the right to satisfy itself that a visitor is a Master Mason in good standing in a Regular Lodge, the visitor in turn has the right to make sure that the Lodge he has come to visit is itself a Regular Lodge, and he may therefore ask to see its charter. But what if the Lodge is already in session and the only available copy of the Charter is on its walls? It is Etiquette to grant his request to see the Charter; on the other hand it is Etiquette not to disturb the Lodge by going in to fetch it; in such an *impasse* the Etiquette of the Lodge should take precedence, and the visitor should be told that if he wishes to examine the Charter, he must come at another time, and before Lodge is opened.

If a visitor satisfies the committee, and if the visitor himself is satisfied, the visitor as yet possesses no right to enter until after the Worshipful Master has consented; for visiting is a privilege, not a right (to *seek* to visit a Lodge is, however, every Mason's right) and a Master may, for good reasons of his own, refuse admittance to any visitor. If the Master does so refuse, Etiquette requires that he call the Senior Deacon to his side and privately instruct him to go to the Ante-room to instruct the Tiler not to admit the visitor. A visitor may be refused admittance for reasons that do not reflect upon him personally.

According to strict Masonic principles no visitor should ever come to the door of the Lodge except solely *as* a visitor —a Mason desiring to sit in a Lodge and to enjoy its fellowship; if he acts in the capacity of an emissary or as an agent, rather than in his own capacity, he should not come as a visitor except on the Master's invitation and according to arrangements previously made; otherwise he should be denied the privilege of visiting *because* he comes not as a visitor but as an emissary. As an example of a justifiable exclusion for non-personal reasons, imagine the following case: some association or society in the community has under way an enterprise that is foreign or even alien to Masonry, but needs funds and decides to solicit the Lodge; for this purpose it selects as a solicitor one of its own members who happens to be a Mason; if the Master refuses to give a hearing to their case, he ought to refuse admittance to their agent—just as, and in the same spirit, he might refuse to have the matter brought before the Lodge by letter or by a motion.

FLAG OF NATION

It is right and proper that the National Colors shall be displayed in the Lodge room at all assemblies, but they should never be nailed or pasted to the wall, or be laid flat, or be used as bunting or decoration, or be hung below any other flag, or touch the floor. This is the Etiquette of the flag in the Lodge room; in other places, and on other occasions, a Lodge observes the forms of the flag etiquette as adopted by the United States Government.

GIFTS TO CANDIDATES

The question of personal gifts to be presented to Candidates during a ceremony is one now arising in general discussion; it is more or less an innovation because it means that something done in the Lodge is being done by somebody who oftentimes is outside it, or is not even a Mason; until Masonic sentiment has crystallized it will be impossible to find rules of Etiquette to apply. As things now are, it is for the Master to decide, and according to the canons of good taste. In some Lodges presentation of personal gifts is permitted without restraint; in others the Master orders that presentation shall be made after the Lodge is closed; in others no presentations are permitted, friends and relatives being asked to make their gifts in private.

GLOVES

Gloves are not a required item of Masonic clothing generally (though once they were), as the Apron is, but are mandatory for certain officers and for certain occasions. A Marshal is expected to wear them whenever on duty. The officers wear them when walking in formal procession. Each member wears them at funerals and interments, and in funeral processions. They are correct for officers at dedication, consecration and memorial ceremonies, and at installation ceremonies. As a rule officers' gloves are white, and may be of leather and gauntlet in style, with insignia on them; members wear white cotton gloves which are kept laundered and in good repair.

GREAT LIGHTS

The Holy Bible is one of the Great Lights, and therefore in Freemasonry possesses a double sanctity; it is the sacred Book of religion, to be reverenced for that reason; and, as one of the Great Lights, is a sacred symbol. It should therefore be a book well kept, not torn, or its covers loose, or shabby; when opened it should be moved and handled in silence, slowly, with reverence, and only at the required moment—not impatiently and beforehand, as if it were a chore to get gotten done, and over with. When removed from the Altar it should be kept in a repository of its own rather than piled with other accouterments. The Square and Compass, since they rank in honor with it as Great Lights should be handled with equal care and dignity; be of the correct size and design, and be preserved with the Bible when not in use.

HAT (MASTER)

The hat is a symbol of the Worshipful Master's authority; since so, it belongs to his office and he does not look upon it as belonging to his private apparel, so that the question of his wearing it does not lie in his personal taste or convenience but belongs to Etiquette. If he removes it during prayer, or at other times when ceremony demands, he is still in a true sense "wearing" it, because it has the same significance when he is holding it as when it is on his head. Whether it is a formal hat or an informal one, it is for the custom of the Lodge to decide; if it is an informal one it is of a style and material that may be worn with good taste.

INFORMATION ON ETIQUETTE

If a Master is in doubt as to the correct form of Etiquette for some particular occasion he has a number of sources of information on which to draw. He may confer with his older members as past officers who usually have had experience of the kind of occasion involved. He may consult a Grand Lecturer, District Grand Lecturer, or other Grand Lodge or District Ritualistic officers; the forms of Etiquette are not confined to the Ritual, yet it belongs in general to the same field and experienced Ritualists usually are well informed on Etiquette. He may consult Masonic Handbooks; and often will find directions for Etiquette in his Monitor, or in a Grand Lodge book of Masonic ceremonies, etc. If he has access to one of them he will find a few books on Masonic Etiquette, though often they are too general in treatment to be useful for questions of detail, but are nevertheless valuable in giving general rules and principles.

INQUISITIVES

A Mason is approached by a man who accosts him thus: "Say, I understand you are a Mason. What do you people think (or do) about so-and-so?" The private Etiquette of a Mason indicates clearly what his answer (in substance) will be: "We have our own private affairs. Nowhere do we take part in activities other than those. They are private and therefore I have not the liberty to discuss them." There is in this inquisitiveness one point: no outsider holds any right either to request, or to demand, information about Masonry; if an outsider becomes inquisitive a Mason refuses to answer, and is under no obligation other than the amenities incidental to any contact between one man and another.

LADIES AT LODGE AFFAIRS

Ladies accepting an invitation to a formal Masonic occasion, reception, banquet, dance, etc., come as guests of the Lodge or of its members. If they are not accompanied by Masonic escort, a Mason, or a committee of Masons, should be at the door to receive them, to conduct them to the meeting room, and later to introduce them among other guests.

If a lady is among men at a social occasion, and without male escort of her own, she needs that a man shall give her his escort and make introductions, and is affronted if left to find her own way about. If she is among men at a Masonic occasion she knows that Masons have customs and an Etiquette of their own, and under such circumstances is doubly embarrassed if no escorts or introductions are provided.

LANDMARKS AND ETIQUETTE

A Landmark is some principle, law, or usage which belongs to Freemasonry and is itself such that if it were to cease Freemasonry would cease with it; "to observe the Ancient Landmarks," therefore, is only another way of saying: "Do not act in such a way as to destroy Freemasonry." Among the Landmarks are a number which involve certain of the usages of etiquette, and involve them so vitally that if the etiquette is not observed the Landmark is violated. In addition to that, Masonic Etiquette as a whole, in its own fundamental principle, is itself a Landmark; if it were to drop out of Masonry, Masonry itself would first deteriorate, then disintegrate, and finally would cease to exist. A Master is the officer whose first duty it is to see that nothing is ever done to harm or destroy the Lodge which is his care; for that reason he can never tolerate a slovenly practice of etiquette, and still less a complete lack or ignoring of it. Since Masonic Etiquette has in it the power and authority of a Landmark none of its observances are meaningless forms and hence it is never to be either lightly regarded or disregarded. If, upon coming to the East, a Master finds that slovenliness and a general indifference in Etiquette have crept into the Lodge he ought to find an early opportunity to address his officers and members on the subject.

LETTERS TO GRAND OFFICERS

In communications addressed to the Grand Master, District Deputy Grand Master, Grand Secretary, or other

Grand Officers, or the Chairmen or members of Grand Committees, which are not personal or private, and which call for official reply, Etiquette requires that they be addressed in full and correct form. Even though a Grand Officer may be an intimate friend this rule is binding because, since the letter calls for official action, it may be referred to other Grand Officers, will go into an official file, may even appear afterwards in printed records, in which event personal familiarity is out of place. It is also a courtesy to a Grand Officer to include in the letter the writer's Lodge, its name, number, address, and also possibly its District, and the writer's own position in it, whether as member, officer, past officer, or committeeman. Since there are many Lodges in a Grand Jurisdiction no Grand Officers can carry each and every one in his memory; to include such data in the letter may therefore save him the time and trouble of looking it up—also may, in so doing, and the point is sometimes important, make possible a more prompt reply.

In some instances a letter addressed to a Grand Master or to a Grand Secretary may contain matter which will affect another Grand Officer or will be of special interest to him; in that event a carbon copy may be mailed to the latter; when such is done, the correct form is to append a postscript to the letter to that effect, in this form: "A copy of this letter has been sent on this same date to so-and-so." If a member of a Lodge writes a letter in which the matter ought, in courtesy, to be known to a Worshipful Master, a carbon copy is mailed to him and the fact is noted in a postscript of the original letter.

MEMORIAL SERVICE IN LODGE

A Lodge can hold each year a memorial service of its own for its Masonic dead, with especial reference and respect to Masons who have died during the year. The service should be tiled and it should be in each detail a *Masonic* service, wholly prepared and carried out by the Lodge itself and not in association with other organizations. A Lodge of Sorrow is not in an official sense a "Lodge"; the ceremony is not a Lodge Communication; but the word, "Lodge" nevertheless denotes the purpose of it, which is to have the members meet as a body to lament the loss of members from that body and to keep them in memory. A Lodge room oftentimes is not equipped, or perhaps is not large enough, to house such a service: if so, it can be held in a church; and it perhaps would be best held in a church in any event, not because it is a religious ceremony, which it is not, but because it is a Masonic ceremony of a type which can be most conveniently held in a church, and will there be in the atmosphere most appropriate to it.

NON-MASONS AT MASONIC MEETINGS

On Masonic occasions where non-Masons are invited, there are three rules of Masonic Etiquette in application: (1) Non-Masons are not asked or expected to participate in any ceremonies or formalities which are themselves Masonic. (2) The non-Masons are present as guests; the Masons are the hosts; the guest-host relationship is therefore observed. (3) There are some usages of Etiquette which belong to esoteric Masonry, and are never employed when non-Masons are present; other usages are not esoteric and such of these may be employed as are appropriate and at the discretion of the Worshipful Master or other officer in charge—the forms of precedence observed in Masonic processions, for example, are non-esoteric and may be used when non-Masons are present and at a Masonic banquet when ladies are guests.

OBJECTIONS FROM THE FLOOR

If a member from the sidelines believes himself to have good cause to object to something that is occurring, or believes that something said or done wrongs himself or another, or questions the right or legality of something said or done, etc., etc., the circumstances may be too exceptional for any general rule to apply, but in most instances the Etiquette for the member to observe consists of: (1) He rises and salutes the Master. (2) He waits until the Master salutes and recognizes him. (3) He states his objection, criticism, etc., in as few words as possible. (4) He salutes and is seated. (5) The Master makes reply or takes action. (6) The proceedings are resumed. In any such event it is not for a member himself to decide or to take action, for that belongs to the Master; the member himself is finished with the episode when he has spoken and re-seated himself; for similar reasons the member is content with merely stating his objection and does not elaborate or discuss it, unless requested to do so by the Master.

INSIGNIA USES AND ABUSES

Certain Grand Lodges have enacted rules to govern the personal wearing or other private use of Masonic insignia—wearing the square and compasses on the lapel, ring, or watch fob, etc.; other Grand Lodges have not enacted any rules at all. In either event the wearing or other use of insignia (as in book-plates, etc.) goes by general consent. But even if it does go by general consent, the violation of certain of the proprieties of Masonic Etiquette is everywhere condemned, and whether a Grand Lodge has enacted rules or not. The principle of Masonic Etiquette in such matters is plain: an insignium does not belong to the Mason wearing or otherwise using it but to the Fraternity, and it may therefore not be so used as to bring the Fraternity into contempt, nor should it be used to bring the Fraternity into contumely by cheapening it. That principle automatically rules out the use of insignia for advertizing or other commercial purposes, or as a personal aggrandisement of the user, or for any similar un-Masonic purpose.

PAST MASONIC OFFICERS

In many societies, fraternities, and clubs an office holder reverts to the same status at the end of his term which belonged to him before. The rule in Masonry, with a few exceptions, is different. Until he is elected to an office a Mason does not have any official status, station, place, or title; but in the case of the majority of offices in a Lodge or Grand Lodge he continues afterwards to hold a well-defined position and a title which is denoted by the word "Past"—a Past Master, for example, has a position and a title and therefore has not returned to the status he held before he was appointed or elected to office. Etiquette recognizes his fact.

What if a Master have among his Lodge members Past Grand Lodge Officers, a Past Grand Master perhaps, a Past District Deputy, etc.? The Grand Lodge itself observes certain rules of Etiquette with regard to them; a Master should observe those same rules in the Lodge.

PAST MASTERS

A Past Master is a Lodge member who has held the highest office in the Lodge but holds no office now; nevertheless, though he is not in an office, he has for life a Masonic position of his own, which has its own identity and recognition and carries with it the title of "Past Master." Past Masters have a standing in Masonic law, in both Lodge

by-laws and Grand Lodge laws or regulations; certain
duties or functions may be assigned to them. In Etiquette
they are entitled to a deference which belongs to their
position, and to a certain order in precedence. On their
own part Past Masters are bound to the same Etiquette
that is observed toward the Worshipful Master as other
members of the Lodge.

PERSONAL VISITS TO MASON

A Mason may call on a stranger who has been reported
to him as a member from another Lodge in another community. To do so belongs to the Etiquette of the Fraternity, and is a courtesy any Mason may be glad to extend
or to receive. When making a Masonic courtesy call a
Brother presents himself at the door as coming on a Masonic visit, makes it clear that he is not there in his private
capacity, and may introduce himself in the name of his
own Lodge, for to do so is a prerogative of membership.
The Brother visited may then converse with him about
Masonry and may give information about his own Masonic
connections.

PETITIONER'S INQUIRIES

It is illegal to solicit men to petition for the Degrees. If
a non-Mason, with the intent to petition, is in search of
information about the Fraternity there are certain facts
which it is lawful to give him, though never with a view to
persuading him to seek membership. The Mason is to
speak for the Fraternity, not for himself; is not to argue
about it; is to be tactful in both silence and speech. That
is the Etiquette, and it is in this instance based on courtesy.
To persuade a man to petition may place that man in an
embarrassing position later on, and one which he himself
could not have foreseen; therefore no Mason, knowing of

that eventuality beforehand, will discourteously lead him into it.

It is proper and highly advisable to let eligible persons, especially De Molays and Builders, know that they must apply and never will be solicited.

PRAYER

Etiquette requires of the Lodge that during prayer it stand and be silent, the officers along with the members, most especially the Master and the Secretary. It requires of the Chaplain that he rise in his own place, wait until the Lodge is silent, move to his position, and speak the prayer with distinction and dignity. He then returns to his place, after which the Lodge is seated. It is a prayer which belongs to Masonry, and should be prepared or learned beforehand, and contain in it nothing of a sectarian character. If, through inadvertence, a Chaplain may include a sectarian expression or phrase, no attention is paid to it, either at the time or among the members after the Lodge is closed.

PREPARATION ROOM

The Preparation Room is sacred to the Candidate and to the officers preparing him; it is therefore necessary that it be closed in and that its privacy is strictly preserved. It is a violation of Etiquette for the Candidate to be under view or made the subject of remarks. The officers preparing him act with dignity and are not expected to discuss with him anything in the Degree he is being prepared for; he, in turn, is expected to obey the officers in charge of him, to make no remarks about them or the preparation, and to ask no questions about the Degrees.

It is proper and advisable to tell the candidate to answer in the same form that questions are asked. For example,

"Is it," etc.? Answer "It is." "Do you," etc.? Answer "I do" instead of "yes, sir" and "no, sir" which sound foolish, and undignified.

PUBLIC APPEARANCE BY LODGES

If in a community activity which is held in public (a parade on Memorial Day, for example) various churches, schools, societies, etc., are asked to participate as a body and to represent their organization, Etiquette requires that a request for a Masonic representation on such an occasion shall be made to the Master, or to the Lodge through the Master, by those responsible, and Masonry cannot be represented unless this propriety has been complied with. Masons in their individual capacity can not represent a Lodge or a Grand Lodge unless they do so by consent or authorization of their Masonic Body or of its responsible Officers.

PUNCTUALITY

A man times his movements on a day in which he expects to attend Lodge according to times set by the Lodge; if the Lodge is unpunctual in opening or closing, his plans made according to the Lodge's closing time are disrupted; in that event he does not look upon unpunctuality in the light of a certain number of minutes on the face of a clock but in the terms of a train, a bus, or an appointment missed; or the discommoding of others who time their movements by him, and he therefore has cause for resentment. Unpunctuality in a Lodge is one of the four or five major reasons for non-attendance; no Mason resents sitting for fifteen or thirty minutes longer in a Lodge but he resents having his plans needlessly disrupted.

Lack of punctuality is a major evil especially in large cities, where members may live at a distance in the suburbs.

Some Masters in such cities cope with the problem of closing time when Degrees are to be conferred by working out a time schedule covering each individual portion of a Degree, so many minutes for opening, so many for the obligation, and so on forth; since some portions may be given in a longer or shorter form, and others are wholly optional, he can fix on a reasonable closing time and schedule the Degree accordingly.

QUIET IN LODGE

When during its proceedings a Lodge is disturbed by any officers or members who are conversing, running about, reading a newspaper, rattling papers, etc., the Master gives a tap of his gavel and asks for quiet. If the proceedings are brought to a standstill, until something necessary to the proceedings has been done, and the Master sees that the wait will last for some minutes, he may give a tap with his gavel and say, "Be at your ease." In such an event and in no other case is conversation, roving about, etc., within the bounds of decorum.

REBUKE

If it becomes necessary for a Master to rebuke a member who has been unruly he may do so after the Lodge is closed, in person, and in private. If it is required that a rebuke be administered while the Lodge is in session, the method to be used is in the Master's discretion but the Etiquette required of him is that he shall administer it in a manner so as not to attract attention to himself or to the member or so as to create a disturbance.

RITUAL ETIQUETTE

The Etiquette governing the conferring of a Degree is both strict and stern: There shall be no laughing, no occasion made for mirth. There shall be no conversation, needless moving about, no disturbances. The officers participating shall never step out of their parts, to hold conversations, to make private remarks, to indulge in asides or in pantomime, or to make remarks about the candidate. Nothing outside the Standard Work shall be substituted for any portion of it. If costumes are worn they must be correct and appropriate. Detailed arrangements must be completed before the degrees begin and not improvised while the Degree is in progress.

SPEAKING FOR MASONRY

A Mason is not entitled, by the mere fact of his membership, to speak in the name of the Fraternity in public addresses. Nor should he ever speak for his Lodge in an interview to be published in newspapers; all statements made in the name of a Lodge for newspaper publication must either come from the Master himself or be made under his direction or with his authority. When a Mason, under legitimate circumstances, and assuming him not to be an official spokesman, speaks or writes for the public on Masonry, the private Etiquette of a Mason dictates that he owes it as a courtesy to the Fraternity to make it clear to his audience that he speaks in his own name only and under his own responsibility.

It is not often that a Masonic officer speaks officially in public, or to the public in the name of the Lodge or the Grand Lodge; when he does so, it should be prepared beforehand and a report made to the Lodge or the Grand Lodge for entering in the records. In such an event Etiquette requires the exact opposite of that required as described above; the speaker makes it clear that he speaks not in his own name but in the name of the Masonic body which he represents. It does not follow that because a

Mason is an officer of a Lodge he is thereby entitled to speak for it; the duty and prerogative of speaking in the name of the Lodge belongs exclusively to the Worshipful Master.

SPEAKER IN LODGE

If a speaker appears at the request of the Lodge the Master is by Etiquette required to make sure that he is met at the airport, train, or bus, or at some specified time and place if he comes in his own car: that accommodations are provided for his entertainment: that he is called for and conducted to the Lodge: that he is given a seat in the East: that he is introduced by the Master, and that such information shall be given about him as will enable the Lodge to feel acquainted with him before he begins his address: that the Master will remain at his side after the Lodge is closed: that he be escorted to his hotel, or his train, that the Lodge shall, at a subsequent meeting, adopt suitable resolutions of thanks, a copy of which should be mailed to him by the Secretary.

SYMBOLS AND EMBLEMS IN LODGE ROOM

The symbolic furnishing or equipment of the Lodge room belong not to the room, in an architectural sense, but to the work of the Lodge in its Communications and in conferring the Degrees. They are without meaning, or use, if not of the correct design and shape and in the right place or order. The Altar stands in the center of the Room, its sides parallel with the sides of the room. The letter G is above the Master's chair; its conspicuous position and its importance call for its being of sufficient size not to be dwarfed by the wall; of a correct and pleasing design, kept in good order, and if illuminated it should be by indirect or by concealed lighting. The Imperfect Ashlar stands

near the northeast corner of the Master's platform, the
Perfect near the southwest corner, and each should be of
stone and large enough to be seen across the room. The
Two Pillars stand in front of the Entrance to the Preparation Room, each on its own pedestal, and away from the
wall, the one bearing the Celestial Globe at the Candidate's right when he enters between them. The appurte-
nances of the Middle Chamber Lecture are often handled
and are large and conspicuous, and therefore need to be
of durable material, correctly designed, and expertly exe-
cuted. The Etiquette of these and other symbolic equipment, like that of the Apron, is largely in the care they
receive and in the manner in which they are handled.

SUNDAY OBSERVANCE

A Lodge cannot hold any sort of Lodge Communication
on Sunday, to transact business or to confer Degrees, but
in a given Grand Jurisdiction it may assemble and open
the Lodge for one or two special purposes, and usually on
a dispensation from the Grand Master. A Lodge may hold
a Memorial Service for its own dead on a Sunday, or may
conduct a funeral service, or may meet for some other purpose of a like kind; the rules in force by the Grand Lodge
govern such occasions and a Master will be guided by them.
But the question which he may not find it as easy to decide
is whether his Lodge shall hold, or participate in, occasions
of another kind: for example, is it suitable for a Lodge to
have a picnic on Sunday? Since the point oftenest at issue
in such questions is one of religious scruple, the Master
may guide himself by the church customs of his neighborhood; what the Protestant Churches do usually would be
suitable, and granting that there are no Masonic rules to
the contrary, for a Lodge to do. It is a matter of fact that
Lodges here and there, more especially in the large cities,

do have outdoor social affairs on Sunday, perhaps in a grove or on a beach; Masonic good taste must decide. There are outdoor occasions of another sort, however, about which in Masonry queries, or questions of good taste, will arise; thus, a Lodge may hold a speaking program of an appropriate kind outdoors; or certain sorts of patriotic programs; or it may go on an automobile pilgrimage to some Masonic shrine, to visit a Masonic Home, etc. In some Grand Jurisdictions Lodges are not only permitted, but are encouraged, to pay Sunday afternoon or evening visits to communities where a number of Masons reside but have no Lodge of their own, to hold an informal Masonic assembly. In general, if the "Sunday question" arises, a Master will be safe if he guide himself, (1) by the customs and taste of his own Lodge and of his community; (2) by Grand Lodge rules; and (3) if in doubt he will consult the Grand Master, Grand Secretary or other Grand Lodge officers.

TARDINESS

If a Worshipful Master is tardy in opening the Lodge through his own dilatoriness, the members are entitled to a word of apology. If he is tardy because of conditions over which he had no control they are entitled to a word of explanation. If an officer's tardiness has delayed the opening, he offers an apology or explanation to the Master before going to his station. If the Master sees that the Closing will be extended to an unreasonable or inconvenient hour, he may announce the fact at some appropriate moment and express himself as willing to excuse any *brethren* who ought not to remain.

TITLES IN MASONRY

In American Grand Jurisdictions there are one or two versions of the uses of each Masonic title; the correct form for any given Grand Jurisdiction can be found in a volume of its Proceedings, usually under the head of "Roster of Officers." In the majority of Grand Jurisdictions the tableau of titles runs as follows:

The Grand Master has the title of "Most Worshipful." This is written or printed in full, or it may be abbreviated in the form M∴W∴A Grand Master is not addressed "Grand Master of the Grand Lodge of the State of ————." but as "Grand Master of Masons in the State of————."

A Past Grand Master has the same title but not in its full form; he is not "Past Grand Master of Masons, etc.," because there may be a score of other Past Grand Masters. He is addressed in a letter as: "M　W∴A.B.C., Past Grand Master, Grand Lodge of————."

The larger number of elective and appointive Grand Officers, along with chairmen and members of a number of Grand Lodge Committees, including Grand Representatives, carry the title of "Right Worshipful"; abbreviated as R∴W∴In some instances such a title is permanent; in others it is valid only for the term in office.

The Master of a Lodge has the title "Worshipful"; abbreviated as W∴A letter is addressed to him in the form: "A.B.C., Worshipful Master, Blank Lodge, No. 1" at such-and-such an address; the salutation is: "Worshipful Sir." He may be referred to in the third person, and when his Lodge title is not given as: "W∴Blank," In some Grand Jurisdictions "Past Master" is considered to be a title; in others it is a designation; usually it is written: "P.M." The title of any Mason, not in an office, is "Brother;" abbreviated as: "Bro." This title is employed in Lodge whenever a Mason is addressed or referred to, it being considered a breach of etiquette to address or refer to him as "Mr. Blank," or "Blank."

TITLES WHEN USED

A Master's title of "Worshipful Master" is in his own Lodge, or in any other Lodge or Jurisdiction, an official title, and wherever he goes it is entitled to recognition as being an official one; thus, if his own Grand Lodge is in Annual Communication his title gains him an unchallenged admittance to the floor; if he visits another Lodge, it receives the deference due to his rank. But if a Master is a member in a body of another Rite, the Royal Arch, the Consistory, etc., or if, as a member of one body, he is a visitor in another belonging to the same Rite, his title has no official standing there (no such body has an office of Worshipful Master) but goes by courtesy only. The converse is true when in turn an official from a body in another Rite visits a Lodge or sits in it as a member; his Royal Arch title (or Knight Templar, etc.) has no official standing but goes by courtesy only. If however an officer of a body in one Rite is introduced as a visitor in a body of another Rite, the Etiquette of Masonic Courtesy requires that his title be used in courtesy when the introduction is made.

UNUSUAL LODGE CIRCUMSTANCES

In any Lodge an unprecedented circumstance or situation may suddenly arise; one that the Lodge has never encountered before, and hence a Master may be caught unprepared, and know no rules to go by. In each and every case of such unprecedented circumstance there is a general principle for the guidance of the Master: he stops all proceedings; addresses himself to the members and asks them to be at ease; he may then take time for himself to reflect, or he may call an officer or a member to his side for a private consultation, after which he should make and announce a decision; upon which he calls upon the Lodge to resume proceedings.

In most instances Etiquette is not involved; in some instances Etiquette is the substance of the matter. Let it be supposed that a visitor comes from another American Grand Jurisdiction or from a foreign Grand Jurisdiction where Lodge rules and customs differ radically from the Master's own, and that this visitor does something or says something wholly unexpected. In that event the Master does not first address himself to the visitor but to his members; he explains to *them* that the visitor is acting according to rules or customs in vogue in his own Grand Jurisdiction, and thus, by indirection, makes it clear to the visitor in what way he has acted unprecedently in the Lodge; he next addresses the visitor, asks him to do this or that, or, if he must, instructs him to do this or that. If the visitor is not at fault, he should not be embarrassed, and it is the point of Etiquette not to embarrass him.

VISITING SICK, INFIRM, ETC.

When a Mason visits a Brother who is ill, or infirm, or for other reasons is confined to his home, a certain Etiquette is involved which belongs to the individual Mason, for not all Etiquette is for assemblies of the Craft. He will ask for permission in advance, in order to make sure of not arriving at an inconvenient time; will present himself as coming from the Lodge; will begin by bringing the greetings of the Lodge; and will adapt the length of his visit and the nature of his talk to information received from the family. There need be no report made of the visit to the Lodge unless the Brother visited requests that there be, or the visitor believes the Lodge is entitled to news or may wish to tender some official act of courtesy.

WORSHIPFUL MASTER AND ETIQUETTE

What is the place of Masonic etiquette in the Craft? It has no special place. It is observed wherever Masons assemble, or speak, or act in the name of the Craft, and for that reason is described as "Masonic." If it belonged to the Ritual of the Degrees a Master might conceive it to lie outside his responsibility, and hold it to be in the care of the Grand Lodge or Grand Officers; but it is in the Ritual as it is elsewhere, neither more nor less, and in no sense peculiar to the Ritual; a Ritual Inspector, Lecturer, or Grand Lecturer may criticize, consult, confer, advise concerning a Lodge's observance of etiquette in the Degrees but he cannot act officially for the Lodge; the Master has full responsibility for it in the Ritual, as he has elsewhere. Etiquette belongs to the Lodge as a whole, without regard to times, places, or stations, and belongs to what the Lodge is essentially, never being anything merely ornamental or formal. Hence the Master is the master of the Lodge's etiquette in the same way and for the same reason that he is Master of the Lodge. It is as much his duty to govern the Lodge in etiquette as in its business, its balloting, its debate, its conferring of Degrees.

CHAPTER VIII

MASONIC FINANCES

I

FUNDS OF THE LODGE
AND GRAND LODGE

MASONRY is not for sale; nor are the rights and privileges of its fellowship ever put up for bidding. When a man pays an Initiation Fee he is not purchasing the Degrees. Masonry is not a business matter; when a member pays his annual dues he is not purchasing shares. It is not itself an object of charity; when a Mason pays fees and dues he does not "give" something, but—and it is a very different matter—he *defrays* something. Masonry pays its own way, meets its own expenses; dues, fees, and assessments are its means to do so. If it were in a world where rents did not have to be paid, where light and heat could be had for nothing, where every letter could go franked through the mails, and food and regalia were to be had for the asking, Masonry could go on without charging dues to its Members or fees to its Initiates, because what it now charges *them* is for nothing which belongs properly to *itself,* but for those expenses which go outside itself to landlords and merchants, and for all those needs which it cannot supply itself just as do churches, schools, libraries, museums, and every other organization and society. It is therefore fundamental that the basis of Masonic finance is not in any money value which is to be placed on Masonry itself, for it has none, but on the cost of goods, services, and similar expenses which it must purchase in order to continue to work; the amount of its expenses are the basis on which it calculates its charges against its members, and hence when a member pays dues he is purchasing nothing and is donating nothing but is defraying his proportionate share of those expenses.

These expenses of a Lodge (it also is true of a Grand Lodge and of every other Masonic body) fall under three general heads: (1) Material expenses for buildings, interest, rent, repairs, equipment, food, light, heat, janitoring, postage, etc. (2) Expenses for required Masonic purposes, which no Lodge can avoid or have any choice about—for relief, charity, the Initiation of Candidates, traveling expenses to a Grand Lodge Communication, etc. (3) Expense for Masonic purposes which are optional with a Lodge, depending on its own needs or circumstances, as for banquets, entertainments, etc. Each and every item of legitimate expense comes under the Landmark that Masonic funds go only for Masonic purposes; and at the same time that each expenditure shall be *official,* that is, it must be passed by action of the Lodge, reported back to it, used according to its instructions, and put on record. These records of a Lodge are the books kept by the Secretary and Treasurer; the archives of a Lodge are a permanent file of its correspondence and documents; when an expenditure goes into the record, correspondence or documents attaching to it go at the same time into the archives. A Masonic dollar is never the property of any individual or committee; and each dollar is officially earmarked for a given expenditure at the time or for an expenditure in the future. A Lodge's finances are sound only if the grand total of its members are defraying the grand total of its expenses year by year.

II

GRAND LODGE FINANCE

THE financial setup of a Grand Lodge is the same as that of a Lodge with only one difference but this difference is fundamental. Where a Lodge calculates its expenses on the basis of members, a Grand Lodge calculates its expenses on the basis of Lodges. What members are to a Lodge, Lodges are to it. Lodges are constituents of their own Grand Lodge; it is not as if a Grand Lodge were a separate and independent organization, and each Lodge were a separate and independent unit. The Lodges in a given Grand Jurisdiction carry on *collectively* the Masonic activities in that State; the Grand Lodge is the means employed by them to do so; and the sovereignty and authority which belong to it are such as are required by it for that purpose. If it incurs expenses it is because the Lodges collectively have incurred them. Since each particular Lodge is responsible for a certain portion of Grand Lodge expenses, what it owes to Grand Lodge each year is equal to the amount of that portion.

The proportion of Grand Lodge expenses chargeable to a given Lodge is calculated on the basis of one or another of two classes of Grand Lodge expenditures: (a) those which are incurred in the same amount by each and every Lodge; (b) those which are incurred by a Lodge in proportion to the number of its members.

In the first class, it is obvious that certain Grand Lodge expenses are the same whether a constituent Lodge is large or small. A small Lodge has as many representatives in a Grand Communication as a large one. It costs as much postage for the Grand Secretary to write to a small Lodge as to a large one. When a Grand Master, a Grand Secretary, or a District Deputy Grand Master, serves a Lodge his time and expenses are usually as much for a Lodge of 50 members as for one of 500; where each Lodge occasions an expenditure equal to each of the other Lodges the allocation of expenses goes equally to each Lodge. Any given Lodge counts as one; never more or less than one.

Under the second class, there are other Grand Lodge expenses which go according to the size of Constituent Lodges. If a Grand Lodge maintains a Home, a Hospital, or a general Relief Fund, their expenses are allocated among the number which receive aid. Other things being equal it is plain that a Lodge of 500 members is likely to have many more who receive aid than a Lodge of 50.

If therefore a Lodge pays annual dues to the Grand Lodge, a portion of each Initiation Fee, fees for Charters and Dispensations, and Assessments for special purposes, they represent the Lodge's proportionate share in the expenses of maintaining a Grand Jurisdiction (there could be no local Lodge if there were not a Grand Jurisdiction); and that share is calculated partly on the basis of equal amounts per Lodge and partly on the basis of a share proportionate to the number of Lodge members.

III
THE ORIGIN OF LODGE EXPENSES

IN a social club the members themselves can decide what activities they will engage in, and how many, and on what scale—a card club can meet once a week or once a month, a fishing club can maintain such quarters as it pleases, an entertainment club can have what parties it chooses and on what scale it can pay for, etc. A Masonic Lodge is not a club but is an Order. If it continues to work it must carry on a number of fixed activities and in a prescribed manner; its members can not choose to carry them on or choose not to. Since this is true the sources of a Lodge's expenditures are easily ascertainable because they are fixed, and are the same in each and every Lodge.

1. A Lodge has a share in Grand Lodge expenditures. Unless it defrays that share it cannot retain its Charter.

2. It also has expenses in its own jurisdiction. There is no way for it to avoid its Masonic duties and obligations to that jurisdiction. Proportionate to the population it will be its duty to receive a certain number of Candidates. Based on the size of its Masonic membership goes its obligation to extend relief to a certain number each year, and that amount will also include relief to sojourners, and courtesies to Master Masons resident near it but not members of it. A jurisdiction is itself thus a source of expense and this is one of the fixed factors in a Lodge's scale of expenditures.

3. It must initiate Candidates. That Candidates are a distinguishable and separate source of expenses is obvious; if it costs money to

hold a Communication, and if three Communications must be called to confer Three Degrees on one Candidate, then that Candidate is the occasion of the expenses of those three Communications. The charging of a Fee for Initiation is a recognition of that fact.

4. A Lodge must have a Room to meet in. A Room means rent or its equivalent, heat, light, equipment, furniture, janitoring.

5. A Lodge must have Stated or Regular Communications at fixed times and Special Communications as needed. Each Communication is a source of expense.

6. Masonic Relief. If Charity is defined as a voluntary form of assistance, given as the donor may choose, when and how, and how much, and the recipient receives it as a bounty on which he had no legal claims, then there is no Charity in Masonry. It is expected, however, that a Mason may fall into misfortune, through no fault of his own, and that his Brethren will feel it a Masonic duty to assist him to the "length of their Cable Tow," not because he is an "object" of charity but because he is a fellow Mason. To do so belongs not only to the Obligations of a member but also to those of a Lodge; there can be no question whether it be an obligation or not because if a Lodge were to refuse its Masonic duties of Relief it would forfeit its Charter; for that reason, Relief is a fixed source of Lodge expenditures.

The above sources of expenditure are fixed and unavoidable. There are other sources, within Masonic purposes, not fixed, but normally to be expected, and depending on circumstances and conditions; these are the expenses of entertainment, of Masonic educational activities, of Masonic funerals, and of occasional calls for community service, etc.

Thus there are clearly defined sources of expenditures which are either fixed and therefore unavoidable, or else which it is not desirable to avoid. But within any given class of expenditures there is a scale which may be high or low. A Lodge must have a Room; that is unavoidable and not for it to decide; but what Room? shall it cost $50 per month for rent or $500? If it have a Lodge banquet shall it be at thirty-five cents a plate or at ten dollars? This scale goes according to the circumstances and conditions of a given Lodge and therefore can not generally be fixed or closely predicted; nevertheless a principle runs through these variations from Lodge to Lodge and it is easy to find it in any given case. There is a saying that a man ought not to marry a woman "unless he can keep her in the style to which she is accustomed." That is an illustration of the principle in question. If a Mason analyzes the Budgets of thousands of Lodges spread over the whole Country he will find that their scales of expenditure differ extraordinarily—one Lodge meets in a room over a store at a monthly rental of $10.00, another meets in a Temple of its own that cost a million dollars; the furnishings in one Lodge Room are threadbare, in another they are luxurious; nevertheless he will see emerging from these various details the general rule that a Lodge's "scale of living" usually represents, on an average, the comforts and conveniences to which its members are accustomed at home, in their work, and in the community.

In view of the fact that there are certain fixed origins of Lodge expense, and that a Lodge's scale of expenses goes according to the general scale of living in its own community, it is not difficult to arrive at a just estimate of a total annual budget of expense which can be taken as normal for that Lodge. What a Lodge's size is, what its jurisdiction is, and the "scale of living" to which its members are normally accustomed; once these facts are seen the mystery vanishes out of Lodge finance and no Master or member need feel uncertainty as to what financial demands are to be made of a Lodge and of its members. If the budget as a whole is thus determined, each particular class of expenditure is determined at the same time, because it is in some fixed proportion to the whole.

Usually in any lodge there is a bookkeeper or accountant familiar with such matters and he should be consulted or placed on the Budget Committee and his advice carefully considered and followed.

IV

INITIATION FEES, ASSESSMENTS, ETC.

A LODGE in a community charges an Initiation Fee of $30.00; another Lodge in that same community, and perhaps meeting in the same building, charges $50.00. It cannot be assumed that one of these Lodges has undercharged its Candidates by giving them a bargain, or that the other has wantonly overcharged its own Candidates in order to swell its treasury. There is a basis on which each and every Lodge calculates the Fee and it is just because the basis is the same for each Lodge. What is that basis?

1. A Lodge is compelled by Masonic law to confer the Three Degrees on each Candidate, with a certain interval between any two of them.

2. To confer a Degree at a Regular (or Stated) Communication usually takes up about two-thirds of the time; if a Degree is conferred at a Communication called expressly for that purpose the Degree takes up the full time.

3. The calling of a Communication entails a certain expenditure each time, and if a Degree is conferred then either the whole, or some portion, (about two-thirds) of that expenditure can be charged against a Candidate. If therefore the total cost of holding Lodge Communications throughout a year be added together then a certain proportion of that total cost can (in theory) be charged against the conferring of Degrees; if this annual cost of conferring Degrees is divided by the number of Candidates of that year, a basis is found for computing the amount of the Initiation Fee, providing that the portion of the Fee which must be sent to the Grand Lodge is taken into consideration and deducted. This method of calculation sounds on the face of it, like a commercial estimate but in reality it is the exact opposite; for it presupposes that the Fee is the Candidate's share of the expenses occasioned by the conferring of Degrees, and therefore does not presuppose that the Fee represents an admittance charge or a price set on Masonry. And since each Lodge has its

own *scale* of expenditures (one paying $30.00 per month for rental of its Room and another $100.00 etc.) the Initiation Fee varies from Lodge to Lodge according to that scale.

Under the principle that Lodge dues and fees are in the long run calculated on the basis of Lodge expenditures, and that these expenditures are in more-or-less fixed categories of regular Lodge activities, no provision is made for calculating the amount of dues and fees for emergency, or extraordinary, expenditures. A Lodge Room may be damaged by a flood, or a fire, or an earthquake to an amount above its insurance; or it may be unexpectedly forced to vacate its premises and thus have the expense of moving;—any number of such contingencies may arise. Therefore when they do arise they are by their own nature of a kind which sets them apart from ordinary, predictable, day-by-day expenditures, and since they are thus emergent the means to raise funds to meet them must also be emergent or special. The usual method is for a Lodge to vote an appropriation in a lump and then to levy an assessment on each member for his prorated share or else appropriate a sum from the Lodge treasury. This power of levying an assessment and of voting funds for such purposes is obviously one that could be easily abused, therefore Grand Lodges have adopted rigorous rules to govern it. Most Grand Lodges forbid any assessments. Many of them have established a minimum fee for the degrees and a more or less uniform Initiation fee for lodges having concurrent jurisdiction to forestall competition for candidates.

V

LODGE BUDGETS

A

IF a budget is a method to make sure that out of the total lodge income a given proportion shall be used by each function of activity during the year, the facts discussed in the above pages would appear to make a budget unnecessary to a Lodge because Lodge funds would seem to budget themselves: the building must be maintained in any event, current expenses are more or less fixed, the expense of initiating Candidates is determined by the number of Candidates, etc. This is partly true. In a basic sense Lodge funds tend to budget themselves; yet at the same time any Lodge has a certain large margin of choice in the total amount it expends, and in fixing the proportions which go to each department, and that choice comes about for two reasons: first, a Lodge can determine the *scale* of its activities, as when it may choose to use a Room at $10.00 a month rental instead of $50.00; second, there are a number of activities which are in accord with Masonic purposes and yet are optional—a Lodge may have ten banquets a year, or one; or more. The usefulness of a budget comes in at the point where a Lodge has this power of choice in expenditures; it is a means for the Lodge to decide at the beginning of the year how much money it will expend during the year, and in what proportions its funds will be divided among the various departments or activities.

But whether expenses are optional or not, they are naturally divided into a number of kinds, or departments, of Lodge activity. No hard and fast line of division can be drawn between one department and another, the line cannot be carried down to the last ten cent piece, but that does not vitiate a budget, which has necessarily a certain elasticity in it. These departments may be called by different names; they are however generally recognized to come under these general heads:

1. Building maintenance. This covers rent, or interest on borrowed money, heat, light, repairs, equipment, janitoring, etc.

2. Current Expenses. This covers postage, printing, secretarial fees, traveling expenses, telephone, etc.

3. Masonic Relief. Relief to members, to sojourners, contributions to community charities and activities, etc.

4. Grand Lodge Dues. This covers Grand Lodge dues, fees, assessments—usually a fixed sum.

5. Masonic Entertainment. For dinners, entertainments, lunches, programs, etc., and expenses incidental to them.

6. Masonic Education. For Masonic speakers, moving pictures, study clubs, etc., and expenses incidental to them.

7. Equipment and supplies. This covers dishes, cooking utensils, linen, aprons, regalia, printed forms, record books, files, etc.

8. Miscellaneous. An emergency may arise calling for an extraordinary expenditure, or the Lodge may embark on some activity unexpected at beginning of year, or there may be items not included in other departments, therefore a contingent fund.

PROCEDURE FOR ADOPTING A BUDGET

B

The adopting of a Budget is an official Lodge action and therefore follows a fixed procedure.

1. The question of adopting a Budget is presented at a Regular Communication one or two months before the close of the fiscal year, and is explained, discussed, and voted upon.

2. If the Lodge votes to adopt one, a Budget Committee is required, and it may be created and named from the floor, or its creation may be referred to the Master. The Master may appoint himself and his officers; or the Treasurer, Secretary, and one other number (preferably an auditor or accountant); In general experience the best type of Committee appears to be the one composed of the Master and his Officers.

3. The Committee draws up the form of Budget which it deems best for the Lodge; calculates the total of income expected and of total expenditures anticipated; divides the Lodge activities into departments; calculates the portion of the fund which ought to go to each Department; embodies the whole in a Report, and presents it to the Lodge at the next Regular Communication.

4. If the Lodge approves the Report that is equivalent to adopting the Budget.

5. Once adopted, the Lodge may then either continue the Committee as a Standing Committee for the year, or else it may appoint the Treasurer and Secretary to act as a Standing Committee. The Budget must be administered; records must be made in it after each Regular Communication; reports on it must be made to the Lodge when called for.

6. Re-apportionment of funds cannot be made except by Lodge action. If a department is over-drawing its apportionment or is leaving its funds lie idle, that fact should be reported to the Lodge.

HOW TO CALCULATE A BUDGET

C

The method most often used for calculating a budget is as follows:

1. A Lodge's income is from dues, fees, assessments, bequests, income from endowments, gifts, and possibly from such sources as admittance charges at entertainments, etc.; the total can be roughly estimated.

2. Subtract from the total amount of expected income any sums that must be set aside for a Savings Fund, Sinking Fund, etc., and they can not be used for Lodge activities. The remainder is the total amount available for budgeting.

3. Average the annual expenditures for a few years past, two or three, or five; if nothing is expected to call for extraordinary expenditures, that average annual expenditure is a safe basis on which to calculate expenditures for the coming year.

4. An analysis of the books for several past years will show into what departments expenditures tend to fall, and the amount being used by each department. If it transpires that any department has been receiving a disproportionate amount, too much or too little, that disproportion should be rectified in the Budget and carefully see to it that it does not occur again in the future.

FORMS OF BUDGETS

D

There are in general three forms of Budgets. Which one of them is best for a given Lodge must be decided according to its needs and circumstances.

1. Budget by Resolution. There are two forms of "Resolution Budgets": one, where the Resolution is to the effect that a given *percentage* of funds shall be allocated to certain named departments; two, where the Resolution names specific amounts instead of percentages. A Resolution in writing is prepared by a Lodge Officer or some interested member; it states the total amount of funds expected to be available; and it recommends that this amount shall be apportioned to a list of named departments according either to a percentage of expenditures or according to fixed amounts. If the Resolution is adopted it becomes a Budget, and the Master, Treasurer, and Secretary are under obligation by virtue of their offices to see that it is adhered to. If a Lodge is small, if its various departments of activity are running on an even keel, a Resolution Budget may satisfy its needs; if it does, the Lodge is saved from the work and expense of bookkeeping.

2. Short Form of Budget. This Form consists of a set of vertical columns across a sheet, printed or drawn, a particular set of columns being under each of seven or eight heads. Across the page are the amounts apportioned for the year, each amount under the head it is apportioned to. At the end of each month the total expended by a department is set down in the vertical column belonging to the department. When a department needs to see how much of its apportionment it has left, it adds these monthly expenditures together, subtracts the total from the fund appropriated for the year, the remainder being the amount left to it for the remaining months of the year.

A convenient variation of this form is to have the Budget

automatically show the amount of funds on hand in any given department at any given time. Under the head of each department have two vertical columns. In the first column set down the date and the amount spent for the month; on a separate piece of paper subtract this from the funds previously on hand; the remainder is entered in the second column and shows the amount now on hand. If, for example, the Entertainment Department began the year with an appropriation of $500, and if during January it spent $55, then in the first column is written the entry: "January 31: $55"; and in the second column the figure "$445". The bottom figure in the second column is always the amount remaining in the apportionment; any Committee or Officer can thus see by a mere glance at the Budget form how much remains in a given department for the remainder of the year and much figuring and consulting of books and records is thereby avoided.

3. The Long Form. The Long Form is in outline the same as the Short except that it breaks sum totals of expenditures down into details. To return to the example used above: if the Entertainment Committee has spent $55 during January this figure is broken down and the sheet will show that of it $30 was for a dinner, $10 for music, and $15 was for a lunch after Lodge. The Long Form keeps a Budget in the sense that fixed amounts are appropriated for each department and it shows whether or not a department is within its apportionment, but it also keeps books on each department. If the amounts expended within each department are totaled at the end of the year the Lodge knows how much of its income went to banquets, to music, to this, and to that. In large Lodges this entails considerable book-keeping, and lays another burden on the Secretary and the Treasurer who must classify Lodge expenditures each month; but in the experience of Lodges which use it, it appears to justify the labor, because the Lodge no longer expends its funds blindly, or for things out of all proportion to their importance.

DRAWING BUDGET FORMS

E

Printed budget forms of many types may be found in any office supply store, or can be printed at small cost by a local printer who can use in their composition "printers' rules" which he carries in stock. If a short form of Budget is used a single sheet will be sufficient for a year; if the long, detailed form is used a number of sheets will be needed, depending on how detailed the record is to be kept. They may be kept in a loose-leaf book.

If a short form is used, and is confined to a single sheet, the paper will need to be about 16 inches across and about 12 inches from top to bottom. Decide first on the heads or departments into which the Budget is to be divided. If there are eight of them (as usually there are) draw lines from near the top to the bottom for 16 columns, with every other line a heavy one. Near the top of the page draw two heavy lines about one-half inch apart across from the left edge to the right edge. The heavy vertical line can be carried up through these two, thereby making across the page a row of rectangles ½ inch deep and two inches long. In each rectangle write down the name of the expenditure—Building Maintenance in the first, Current Expenses in the second, etc. Beneath that row of headings draw horizontal lines across the page one-half or three-quarters of an inch apart. Each of these lines will carry the entries for one month.

Immediately beneath each heading write in the amount of funds apportioned to it for the year. At the end of each month write into the first of the two columns under its heading the amount spent by it during the month; on the same line, and in the second column, write in the balance of the apportionment still remaining.

If the Long Form is used the same size of paper will be required but much more space will be required for each month; also three columns will be needed under each heading instead of two. At the end of the month the expenditures of any given heading are broken down into two, or three, or four classes, etc.; each separate class will require a line for itself; if there are, say, three classes of expenditures three lines will be required for the month. In the first column write in the classification; as, for example, rent, janitor, banquet, etc.; on the same line in the second column write the amount of money expended; at the bottom of the various classes of expenditures add up the amounts, subtract the total from the fund remaining in the apportionment as of the end of the previous month, and the remainder is the amount still remaining of the apportionment, this amount can be entered in the third column under the same heading. When all the entries are made across the page one heading will have used up more lines than any other; immediately under it draw a heavy line across the page; the space above that line will give a picture of budget expenditures for the month. If there are 20 lines across the page and if each month required on an average six lines, then one sheet would cover three months, and four sheets will be required for a year.

A budget is of great advantage to a Lodge and is especially useful to the Worshipful Master, the Secretary and the Treasurer.

ADVANTAGES OF A BUDGET

F

1. A Budget sheet is a convenient source of information. It yields facts about the Lodge's funds and expenditures in a minute of time, and often when there would not otherwise be time to hunt through the records. If, for example, a member of a Committee moves at some Regular Communication that the Lodge should purchase some item of equipment, or have an entertainment, or engage a paid speaker, etc., the question is sure to be raised whether the treasury will admit of it, and if it does how much money can be appropriated. If a Budget is in use such facts are instantly available, time will be saved, and the Lodge will not be acting in the dark.

2. A Budget is convenient especially to a Worshipful Master. He is likely to have in mind, or to have under preparation, plans for Lodge activities months ahead. If he can see about how much money will be available it gives him guidance in working out his plans. Moreover, he can always have, without trouble to himself or to the Secretary, an overall picture as of any given date of the financial condition of the Lodge and of the channels along which its expenditures are flowing; he is more concerned than any other officer to make sure that Lodge expenditures are kept in balance.

3. The Budget guarantees first to the Master, and then to the Lodge, that the Lodge shall, during the year faithfully discharge each and every one of its duties, not permitting any one to fall into neglect, or any one to loom too large and thereby work an injustice on the others. If a Lodge is to have entertainments through the year it will not wish to have them at the expense of other Masonic purposes; on the other hand it will not wish its social life to fall below normal by allocating a disproportionate amount of time and funds to another form of activity. So is it with each department of Lodge work; each department has a place of its own in Masonic life, and is entitled to a proportionate share of Lodge funds. If the departments of Lodge's expenditures are in balance, the activities of the Lodge will be in balance, and no member can find fault with it; and at the same time Lodge activities cannot be kept in balance if required funds are lacking. Thus in the long run a Lodge Budget is not alone a system of book-keeping or a method of financing but is a method to prevent a Lodge from failing to carry out any one of its duties as a Lodge, and does it by controlling Lodge expenditures with that end in view.

A budget which is not reviewed from time to time by the lodge officer or some interested and well informed member is as bad or worse than none at all. It should not only be reviewed but its provisions strictly enforced and its limitations rigidly observed.

VI

FINANCING A LODGE BUILDING— AN ADDITION OR REPAIRS

IN the origin of the present system of Speculative Freemasonry two hundred years ago much thought was given to a Lodge's financial structure; and certain financial principles were established in the Fraternity once and for all. This was in England. If today a Mason studies that financial structure he sees clearly that from top to bottom it was based on the principle that a Lodge would have current expenditures (to be defrayed by dues) but no capital expenditures. Lodges were small; many Masons belonged to two or three or more Lodges at the same time; the expenditures of a normal Lodge fell into three categories: (a) rent, heat, light, equipment; (b) cost of holding meetings, dinners, entertainments; (c) relief and charity. The system of fees and dues was worked out on the basis of a small Lodge with those three categories of expenditures; it was not supposed that a Lodge would ever erect a building (why should it?) or would purchase land, buildings, or other properties. Therefore the structure of Lodge finance as finally established had full provision for current income and expenditure; but had no provision for capital investment. Once that structure was established, the rules and regulations, including each member's financial obligations to the Craft, were adjusted accordingly.

Such, in the main, is the Lodge financial structure to this day; and because it is that way the financing of the purchase of a property or the erection of a building invariably calls for devices not originally provided for in the Masonic system. A Board of Trustees must be created expressly for the purpose; or an independent building corporation must be established; or an arrangement must be made for a bank to finance the enterprise; lawyers must be consulted to make sure that the Building Fund Trustees or the Corporation or the Contract shall conform to State laws.

During the decade between 1920 and 1930 American Masonry financed a nation-wide program of new buildings of an unprecedented scope, so unprecedented that in its whole history the Fraternity had never seen anything like it before and is not likely ever to see anything on the same scale again. Some of the lessons learned from that boom period were bitter; others are in the process of being learned; and almost every Grand Lodge has been looking about for some basis, some sound and equitable policy, by which to regulate building projects in the future. What general policy will crystallize out of the experiments and experiences it is as yet too early to predict, with the one possible exception that each Grand Lodge will probably require of every Lodge by law that any new building or investment enterprise must be submitted to it for examination and approval before the Lodge can undertake it.

In the meantime it is advisable to set before one's self a number of principles, Landmarks, and fundamental facts in the light of which it is possible in any given set of circumstances to determine what is wise for a Lodge to do, whether to have a building of its own or not:

1. How does a Lodge decide whether to buy or to erect a building or not? Obviously the most general answer would be that each Lodge must decide the question for itself; if it is financially able, if its members desire a building, there is nothing in the laws or Landmarks to prohibit it. Nevertheless and even so, a Lodge has one definite guidance. If we turn back to our discussion of Lodge Budgets we will recall that the principle underlying a Budget is that a Lodge is required by its Charter to carry on Masonic activities of certain kinds, that these activities involve expenditures, and that the total expenditures are divided among the activities in proportion; unless a Lodge budgets its funds according to that principle it will not be able to carry on the activities required of it by its Charter. One of those Budget Heads covered building costs, rent, interest, upkeep, janitoring, repairs, permanent equipment, etc.; according to the Budget a Lodge is able to apportion

to that Head only a certain percentage of its total funds. This Budgeting principle helps to answer the question as to whether a Lodge can finance a new building: namely, if in order to have a new building a disproportionate amount of current Lodge funds must go under the head of Building to the detriment, or the extinction, of other required activities then the Lodge cannot afford it; if expenses incidental to a new building do not exceed the Budget then a Lodge can afford it.

2. Do the members of a Lodge, the majority of them, and after they have received full information, and been given sufficient time for reflection, really desire a new building, or does the expression of desire come from a small minority of more vocal members? If the nation-wide experience of the Craft is a criterion, including the findings of nearly 16,000 Lodges, over a long period of years, the great majority of Lodges prefer rented quarters to quarters of their own, not always because they cannot afford a building of their own but because they find rented quarters more convenient, more adaptable, and more easily adjustable to the rise and fall in membership and to fluctuations in the financial ability of their members. If a Lodge has nothing but a Lodge Room, an Anteroom, and a Preparation Room, it is not crippled at any point in its Masonic work; if it has a building of its own there is nothing it can add to Masonic work, for additional building space does not alter Masonry and can add nothing except convenience and comfort.

At the height of the building boom between 1920 and 1930 it was everywhere taken for granted that if there were in a town two or three Lodges in addition to one or two in the suburbs these Lodges would be better off if they pooled their resources, and instead of four or five Lodge rooms scattered about the community had one large temple in its center. There was much said in favor of that argument beforehand; and now, after the event, Lodges in many communities find that it worked out as they hoped. But most of these satisfied Lodges meeting in one temple are in the smaller towns and cities; in the larger cities, and especially in the metropolitan centers, the single Masonic Temple is not proving satisfactory in an increasing number of cases, and for these reasons: (a) Lodges lose their feeling of neighborhood. Where they meet is far from where their members live and work. In time they cease to be neighborhood Lodges altogether because, in a city with concurrent jurisdiction, a Petitioner from any part or section of the city can petition any Lodge he chooses. (b) Masonry's influence is not felt in the neighborhood where a Lodge meets; at least it is felt only in an attenuated form. (c) If a number of Lodges meet in the same building the whole leadership and guidance of the Craft for a large community tends to fall into the hands of a small circle of men. (d) Members attending from outlying districts must spend too much time going and coming, return home too late at night, and are put to extra expense—for example, they may have to eat their dinner in restaurants in order to be on time at Lodge, etc. (e) In the long run, and on the average, it costs more for a Lodge to have quarters in a large Temple than in local rooms. (f) Attendance is not as large in proportion to membership in central Lodges as in neighborhood Lodges. (g) Nothing is gained for Freemasonry itself by centralization because the Craft has no program of city-wide activities which it would be convenient to operate from one center.

The advantages, on the other hand, are obvious: (a) A Lodge uses quarters expressly designed and built for Masonic purposes. (b) It enjoys conveniences it could not afford for itself. (c) The Craft can have the use of a large auditorium, banquet hall, club rooms. (d) The Bodies of the various Rites can meet under the same roof. (e) A Masonic Temple is a community asset, usable for many purposes other than Masonic, and may be a monumental structure which adds much to the dignity or beauty of a city, and thereby signalizes and embodies the Craft's value to, and its place in, the whole community; to erect a monumental structure is one of the largest of all possible contributions that Lodges can make to their community to which they are so much indebted.

3. When discussing the construction or purchase of a building

there is one fact of such cardinal importance that, if it is ignored or evaded, everything will go awry and the Lodge will be put in the wrong: *What any member contributes to a building is a gift which he makes to the Lodge.* This is true in the nature of the case. Once a building belongs to a Lodge it does not belong, and no part of it belongs, or ever can belong, to any member; a contribution to a Lodge building fund is not an investment, pays no dividends, is not a share of stock, is not transferable, cannot be deeded or inherited, etc. Since a member owns nothing of that for which he pays, the amount he pays is a gift. Furthermore, there is nowhere in the Obligations any requirement of a member, nor among the qualifications of membership any stipulation, that once in Lodge membership a Mason must invest in real estate. If the Lodge votes a capital investment, and if to do so it levies an assessment on each member, the amount given by each member in response to his Lodge's demands is an assessment—it is a forced gift, but a gift nevertheless. Temple company bonds are transferable, or may be inherited, but frequent defaults in interest payments and refusal to redeem them have been very injurious to the Craft.

Gifts, donations, contributions, these are the basis on which a building is financed, and on the basis of which the amount is worked out which each member will be asked to contribute. Manifestly men cannot be expected to *donate* as much money as they might be able or willing to put in an investment; money put out today in an investment should come back in profits; money donated to a building in which a man owns nothing, is money gone forever. A man who might be able to afford an investment of $200.00 might not be able to afford a gift of $50.00. And the point is accentuated by the fact that Freemasonry itself is without price, cannot be bought or sold, can have no money value placed on it, and it may have as much worth for a man in a $30.00 a month room as in a $300.00 a month temple.

Since building contributions are gifts, it is not often that the members of a Lodge can, on an average, give enough for a new building.

Since this is true a Lodge usually must look to a few among its wealthier members to give large sums. If such Brethren give much, they are to be honored; they are sharing their wealth with their Brethren in a dignified way, and to nobody's embarrassment or humiliation; but their contribution, even though it be $100,000.00, is a gift in the same sense, and on the same conditions, as those of other members; they do not own any more in a temple than the less wealthy members because they *own* nothing at all.

4. A building will stand for Masonic uses over a long period of years; it may even appreciate in value as time passes; it is therefore in principle fair to pass on part of the cost to Masons in future years. But on what basis shall the apportionment be made between the charge on present members and the prospective assessment made on future members? Masonic jurisconsults have pondered often over this question but as yet are not agreed among themselves beyond the initial assumption that it is not just to levy on the present generation of members the full cost because they will not enjoy the full use. On the other hand these men must make another assumption and one which comes into conflict with the first: by what right can the present members saddle a debt on members twenty years hence? It is doubtful if any Lodge has financed a new building without having to find a compromise between the members who insist that a part of the debt ought to be passed on to the future and the members who insist that it is unjust to foredoom future members to a debt which has been contracted for them and that without their voice or vote. But the State cuts through this Gordian knot of argument with its laws on contract, and it is with those laws that a Lodge must comply. If the members who belong to the Lodge contract to finance a building those members become *responsible for the full debt* at the moment the contract is signed. It is doubtful whether a Grand Lodge can *forbid* a Lodge to build a temple without invading its sovereignty. Some Grand Lodges have a Temple Building Committee and inform their Lodges they will not *dedicate* a temple unless the plan, specifications and financing have been approved by that Committee.

VII
LODGE DUES

THE amount of dues which a Lodge requires each of its members to pay into its treasury once a year has to be decided according to the circumstances and conditions of each Lodge, and therefore cannot be decided in the abstract, or on a basis of averages. What dues are in themselves, however, and disregarding the amount of them, is the same for Lodges everywhere, and if their nature and purpose are clearly understood it is easy to arrive at a fair estimate of their amount in any given case.

1. In principle, annual dues represent a member's own share in the total Lodge expenditures for the year. Since his share is arrived at by dividing the total expenditures by the number of Lodge members his share is automatically the same as that of every other member, and is not arbitrarily arrived at; and since he has an equal voice and vote in the Lodge he is equally responsible with every other member for the annual volume of Lodge expenditures, and he has no grounds for feeling that he "stands off to one side" and that "they" have decided what he is to pay. Since dues are a share in the total volume of expenditures, the expenditures being made by the members conjointly, then dues are exactly what the name implies, a *share,* and are therefore not fees, or assessments, or a price that is charged, or a form of paid admission. There is in the Lodge no Officer, or staff of Officers, nor any Committee to decide what the dues shall be; they are decided whenever the Lodge as a body decides on activities that involve expense; as a Lodge goes on, month after month, carrying on this activity and then that one, it is in that process deciding what the dues must be, because it is deciding what the volume of expenditures is to be; and since the members decide for themselves what activities they carry on, they decide for themselves what their dues must be. If there are 200 members in a Lodge, and if some night its members vote to purchase a new carpet, and the car-

pet is to cost $50.00, each member in so voting has assessed himself twenty-five cents in dues. He is in debt for that much; if he does not pay that debt in the form of dues some other Lodge member will be paying it for him.

2. As was stated on another page a number of factors enter into a Lodge's annual expenditures. There are fixed charges for building, rent, heat, light, etc. There are Candidates to be Initiated. The Lodge has a certain number of members. It must pay dues and assessments to Grand Lodge. Since it is a Masonic Lodge, it is in duty bound to do certain things; to hold Communications, to give Masonic Relief, to sustain Masonic fellowship, etc.; if it does not discharge these duties it may forfeit its Charter. Its members, on an average, are accustomed to a certain general scale of comfort and convenience, and will expect the Lodge to maintain that scale. There are optional activities which a Lodge may engage in, or not, as its members decide. Out of these facts and factors there emerges in outline a picture, often very clear, of what the normal standard of expenditures is for a given Lodge. If a Lodge be an average Lodge its expenditures will be according to that average standard; and since each member's dues are his proportionate share in that volume of expenditure the amount of his dues will be an average amount. Lodge dues therefore cannot be considered as if they stood apart from Lodge activity as a whole, for it is the character and amount of Lodge activities which of themselves determine how much the dues are; since this is true the only possible means to regulate or adjust Lodge dues is to regulate and adjust Lodge activities. If the dues are too low it is because the Lodge is doing too little; if the dues are too high it is because the Lodge is doing too much. If the members refuse to pay enough dues to enable the Lodge to fulfill its Masonic purposes they are not entitled to have a Lodge; if they are paying too much their Lodge is extravagant and it is for them by their voice, and vote, to bring it to a more reasonable scale of expenditures.

3. In what does a Mason's responsibility for paying dues consist? In the one fact that he is a *member*. By the mere fact of becoming a

member, and without further discussion or assent, he guaranteed to support the Lodge; he approved the Lodge; he made himself a party to its activities; he guaranteed his own share in defraying its expenses. His responsibility for dues does not spring from the fact that he attends Lodge, or takes a voice in it; or is on a Committee; or is an Officer; or "attends Masonic functions"; it springs solely from the fact of his membership. Therefore his responsibility is not affected if he never attends, or takes no part, or moves away. A non-active member's financial duties are precisely the same as an active member's; if consideration be given to the members when a Lodge is calculating its dues no less consideration should be given to him because he is inactive, but neither should any more consideration be given to him. It is specious to argue that because he received little from a Lodge and he does not attend, therefore he should pay less; dues are not payments made in return for benefits or services received but are a *duty* inherent in membership, and that duty remains the same as long as his membership itself remains the same.

CHAPTER IX

LIFE MEMBERSHIPS

"LIFE membership" is in one sense a misnomer because the Landmarks which define Masonic membership and, by implication, define Lodge dues, nowhere include any such arrangement as "life" membership. Membership is conditional on the "good standing" of a Mason; he observes the rules, keeps the laws, is not guilty of conduct unbecoming a Mason; these are Landmarks, but in no Landmark is there such a thing as a fixed term of membership for a year, or a number of years, or for life; nor anywhere is membership expected to be conditioned by any special arrangement between a Lodge and a member, nor is a Lodge expected to set up a special class of members. If a member pays his dues in advance that money does not guarantee him his membership even for one year; he may be suspended or expelled at any time, and when he is, the fact that his dues have been already paid does not exempt him from the penalties of un-Masonic conduct. If annual dues cannot guarantee a man his membership for one year, neither can a large fixed sum paid at one time guarantee him his membership for "life."

In Lodges which grant Life Memberships the Lodge provides in a by-law that if a member so desires the Lodge will enter into a contract with him to itself pay his dues from that time on, and the member in turn agrees to pay for that privilege an amount fixed by the Lodge, $100, $150, $200, etc., as the case may be. The status of that member remains unchanged except that each year it is considered that his dues have been paid in advance by the Lodge out of the earnings of the lump sum payment he made. This arrangement is not supposed to give him any special privileges, but it is argued that if a man can pay his dues for one year in advance he should be allowed to pay them for two, or for ten, or for thirty years.

A number of Grand Jurisdictions, perhaps a majority of them, now permit the financial arrangement called "Life Membership" (though *every* member is expected to be a member "for life"), and some thousands of Lodges have put the plan in practice. From a review of Grand Lodge Proceedings over a period of years it does not appear that the legality and Masonic regularity of the practice have been anywhere seriously questioned; nor does it appear that Lodges have found themselves damaged by it as a trust fund the interest on which will pay the dues each year except where they have used the lump sum for current expenses instead of holding it. Insofar as one can see from general, country-wide experience Lodges have found Life Membership a satisfactory practice in the sense that it has not been condemned as an unlawful practice. Some Grand Lodges prohibit it but recognize the validity of *existing* Life Memberships as they are valid contracts in law.

But even so it is too soon to judge of the scheme because in the nature of the case, the experiment must cover a period of many years. Perhaps by the end of a half century it will have proved itself to be sound in finance and Masonic in its general effects. If the question is to be thus answered by the method of trial and error the answer must wait for some years to come; the scheme is as yet too new for any verdict at the present time. There are, however, an increasing number of Masons, who are well learned in our laws, of a ripe experience in Masonic practice, and whose judgment has weight in their own Grand Lodges, who refuse to consider the "Life Membership question" one of "trial and error," or a problem in book-keeping, or one on which judgment must be suspended for a half century, but insist that the question is one involving a number of Landmarks, and that since the Landmarks are the same now that they will be a half century from now, the question can be decided at any time by Masonic statesmanship. These Masons are convinced that Life Membership is questionable; they have powerful arguments against it. A Lodge and its officers may not agree with those men; its Grand Lodge rules permitting, a Lodge may decide for itself to adopt the scheme and it will be guilty of violating no Masonic laws if it does unless its Grand Lodge forbids it; yet it is wise for such a Lodge to be clear in its understanding of what it is doing, and it and its officers may, to that end, want to give consideration to the arguments against the plan before they vote it into their by-laws.

Imagine that there is a Masonic Supreme Court for American Lodges; imagine that a case involving the principle of Life Membership is brought by a Grand Lodge to that court; imagine that the attorney for that Grand Lodge presents his arguments against it. Such a Supreme Court would have for its own guidance not Grand Lodge rules or Lodge by-laws alone but the whole body of the Ancient Landmarks. The attorney's arguments would therefore be framed to prove that Life Membership is in violation of one or more Landmarks. His arguments would be:

1. There is no Landmark which provides for Life Membership.

2. Life Membership is a scheme whereby if a member pays a large sum fixed by the Lodge he is on that date released from the payment of his annual dues during the years he remains in membership. This scheme is in violation of the principle of Lodge dues, and the violation occurs at a number of points.

(a) The Book of Constitutions provides that each member shall pay dues. The dues are fixed by the Lodge annually. There is nowhere provided a *substitute* for dues. Manifestly if the dues for a given year are fixed at $5.00 a sum of $200, or some portion of $200, cannot be considered to be dues, but is a special financial arrangement made in *lieu* of dues.

(b) Dues are a member's share of the expenditures of his Lodge. Those expenditures are continuous from day to day, and they fluctuate from day to day, and therefore from year to year. Thus, a Lodge which pays out $50 in Relief this year may pay out $500 next year. The member's obligation is a *current* obligation for *current* expenditures; and therefore is in effect, and in principle, wholly unlike a fixed share in a capital investment. If it is impossible for a Lodge to know now what its expenditures will be next year, still less is it possible for it to know what its annual expenditure will be for some date ten years from now, or twenty, or thirty. Since dues are calculated on the basis of actual expenditures, and since the actual expenditures of a year beginning at a date in the future cannot be known, there is no way to tell now what the dues will be then. The sum paid by a Life Member cannot therefore be described as dues because no Lodge can know beforehand what its dues will be at any future date. If the sum paid is not dues, then what is it? Manifestly it is a *substitute* for dues, and since a Life Membership fee is not dues the Life Member is not paying *dues,* and therefore is violating Masonic law.

(c) The Life Membership scheme results in one member paying more or less toward Lodge expenditures than another even if the lump payment be considered a trust fund and only its earnings be used. Suppose that a member may be expected to remain in membership for thirty years; suppose that the average amount of dues for thirty years is estimated to be $5.00 per year; on that scale a Life Member would have paid dues in advance for thirty years if he paid the Lodge $150.00 in a lump sum. But suppose that owing to an era of extremely high prices (as from 1925 to 1930 or 1948 to 1958) the Lodge expenditures over a period of five years amount to $10.00 per member per year; the Life Member therefore is during those years paying only one-half as much as other members. Or suppose that in a period of extremely low prices the expenditures drop to $3.00 per year; the Life Member is then paying $2.00 more per year than other members.

(d) The dues are arrived at by dividing a Lodge's annual expenditures by the number of members. Those expenditures are consented to, or incurred by, the members themselves, sitting in the Stated or business Communications of the Lodge. Thus in the long run, and on an average, each member, as he acts in Lodge, acts to fix the amount of his own dues. But in that same act he is also acting to help fix the dues of each and every other member; for if he votes an expenditure each of the members has a share in it equal to his own. Since a member knows that his own vote helps to assess a sum of money on another member, he will, in voting, give to the other member's financial ability the same consideration that he gives to his own. For him to do so, belongs to the principle of Masonic dues. But if a Life Member is paying no dues he nevertheless acts, by voice and vote, to fix dues for other members and when doing so, needs not to give consideration to his own financial ability. He can vote monies which other members will have to pay but they cannot vote on what he will pay.

3. A Lodge itself receives no financial benefits from the scheme of Life Membership except in case of his death earlier than anticipated. If the Lodge acts on the theory that the lump sum is not dues but a fee in consideration of which dues are remitted; or if it acts upon the theory that the lump sum *is* dues, it must, in either event, use the money for the same purposes as dues; therefore it must prorate the lump sum over a period of years. It cannot use the whole sum at once because most of it belongs to future expenditures; it can therefore use, of it for any year, only that portion which belongs to that year. In any given year the Lodge receives from its Life Member only an amount supposed to represent the dues in that year, and is therefore never a gainer unless he dies shortly after making the payment. It merely must keep a complicated set of books; otherwise it is unaffected. The only gain is to the Life Member, and his gain at most is a very dubious one and at best consists of nothing more than a minor convenience, which he can only enjoy at the expense of his Lodge's inconvenience.

4. It is unjust for the members in the Lodge any year to reach out into the future, when the Lodge will have changed and the majority of present members are gone, to decide by official action what the dues are to be for a future year. By what right can Lodge members

now determine Lodge activities (for dues determine activities) for the Lodge twenty or thirty years from now? It is a fundamental principle in Masonry that Lodge expenditures go for Masonic purposes and are in total amount what those purposes require; what they require is determined as the Lodge goes along from day to day. What they will require at a future day cannot be discovered until that day arrives.

5. The scheme of Life Membership— (we continue to imagine that these are the arguments of a Masonic attorney against Life Membership before a Masonic Supreme Court)—tends to set up a privileged class among the members. Not many members can afford to pay any such sum as $200.00 at one time; this fact is not only recognized but also is advertised by the presence among them of members who are able to do so; a financial distinction is introduced into the very essence of membership. "Over here" are "ordinary members"; over there are "Life Members." This distinction, and it is a distinction which arouses resentment wherever it is made, is a violation of the Landmark of complete equality among Lodge members in respect of the dignity, status, rights, duties, and privileges of membership. Thus might an attorney argue.

As stated before it is too soon to learn from actual practice what the total effects of the scheme of Life Membership are going to be; even so, some experience already is on record and in it are a few illuminating facts. To describe one case only: a certain Eastern Lodge granting Life Memberships had in its membership a number of professional accountants and auditors. While a group of these were discussing Lodge affairs over a lunch table the question of Life Membership arose, and they fell to discussing their own Lodge's scheme from the standpoint of sound actuarial practices; and before they had finished they discovered that their Lodge was charging less than one-half of the amount it ought to charge if it were not to be a financial loser. They raised the question at the next Communication of the Lodge; the Lodge in turn raised it at the Grand Lodge; the Grand Lodge in its turn appointed a Special Committee consisting of Masons from the State Tax Commission and from among life insurance actuaries. After two years, that Committee stated in its Report that Lodges in the Grand Jurisdiction which granted Life Memberships were on an average charging one-third too little, that many of them were using Life Membership Fees in *current expenditures* and not pro-rating them, that no Lodge was discovered to have a book-keeping system such as was required to keep Life Membership accounts. Their Report also showed, at least by implication, that many of the Lodges were confusing the idea of Lodge dues, which come in principle under the general head of current income and expenditures, with the wholly unlike principle of a share of stock in a capital investment. The Report also implied that upon expert analysis a Life Membership fee could not be classified or described as a form of annual dues, therefore it belonged to a class of fees of another kind, and since no Grand Lodge law provided for fees of that kind, the Grand Lodge would either have to provide such a class by legal action or else would have to hold that since a Life Membership fee is not a form of dues the payer of it is not paying dues and is therefore violating the law requiring each member in good standing to pay dues. The only now conceivable method for a Life Membership scheme to conform to Masonic laws would be for a member not to pay dues in advance but to put a lump sum in escrow in some bank and authorize the Lodge to draw on it at the dues paying date for each year a sum equal to the dues for that year. If this plan be adopted then Life Membership would be reduced to nothing more than a device by which a Lodge Secretary would receive a member's dues from a bank instead of from the member himself; in that event, and since no Lodge can guarantee any Mason's membership in the future, the "Life Member" deprives himself of the use and custody of a sizable sum of his own money over a long period of years and receives nothing in return for doing so except to be relieved once a year of signing a check and sending it through the mails—a matter of two or three minutes of time. Presumably the unused portion of this trust fund would pass to the

INDEX

225